ANGELS IN AMERICA

A Gay Fantasia on National Themes

PART TWO: PERESTROIKA

Tony Kushner

D0465705

BROADWAY PLAY PUBLISHING INC
224 E 62nd St, NY, NY 10065
www.broadwayplaypub.com
info@broadwayplaypub.com

ANGELS IN AMERICA:
PART TWO: PERESTROIKA

© Copyright 1992, 1994, 1996, 2013 by Tony Kushner

All rights reserved. This work is fully protected under the copyright laws of the United States of America.
No part of this publication may be photocopied, reproduced, stored in a retrieval system, or transmitted, in any form or by any means, electronic, mechanical, recording, or otherwise, without the prior permission of the publisher. Additional copies of this play are available from the publisher.

Written permission is required for live performance of any sort. This includes readings, cuttings, scenes, and excerpts. For amateur and stock performances, please contact Broadway Play Publishing Inc. For all other rights please contact Joyce Ketay, The Gersh Agency, 41 Madison Ave, NY NY 10010, 212-634-8105.

I S B N: 978-0-88145-652-3

First printing: January 2017

Typographic controls: Adobe InDesign
Typeface: Adobe Caslon
Printed and bound in the U S A

ANGELS IN AMERICA, PART TWO: PERESTROIKA
was first performed as a staged reading by the Eureka
Theatre Company, May 1991.

The world premiere was presented by the Mark Taper
Forum, November 1992

The play was presented by New York University/Tisch
School of the Arts, April 1993

The play opened in London at the Royal National Theatre
of Great Britain in November 1993.

The play opened in New York at the Walter Kerr Theatre
in November 1993.

The first production of ANGELS IN AMERICA, PARTS
ONE AND TWO was presented at the Mark Taper Forum,
November 1992.

THE CHARACTERS
IN *PERESTROIKA*

ROY M. COHN,* a successful New York lawyer and unofficial power broker.

JOSEPH PORTER PITT, chief clerk for Justice Theodore Wilson of the Federal Court of Appeals, Second Circuit.

HARPER AMATY PITT, Joe's wife, an agoraphobic with a mild Valium addiction.

LOUIS IRONSON, a word processor working for the Second Circuit Court of Appeals.

PRIOR WALTER, Louis's boyfriend. Occasionally works as a club designer or caterer, otherwise lives very modestly but with great style off a small trust fund.

HANNAH PORTER PITT, Joe's mother, formerly of Salt Lake City, now in Brooklyn, staying in Harper and Joe's apartment.

BELIZE, a registered nurse and former drag queen whose name was originally Norman Arriaga; Belize is a drag name that stuck.

THE ANGEL, four divine emanations, Fluor, Phosphor, Lumen and Candle; manifest in One: the Continental Principality of America. She has magnificent steel-gray wings.

Other Characters in Perestroika

ALEKSII ANTEDILLUVIANOVICH PRELAPSARIANOV *(pronounced AntedilooviAHNuhvich PrelapsARianohv)*, the World's Oldest Bolshevik, is played by the actor playing Hannah. He should speak with a Russian accent, strong but comprehensible.

MR. LIES, Harper's imaginary friend, a travel agent, played by the actor playing Belize. In style of dress and speech he suggests a jazz musician; he always wears a large lapel badge emblazoned "IOTA" (International Order of Travel Agents).

HENRY, Roy's doctor, played by the actor playing Hannah.

ETHEL ROSENBERG, played by the actor playing Hannah.

The mannequins in the Diorama Room in the Mormon Visitors' Center in Act Three:

THE FATHER, played by the actor playing Joe.

THE RECORDED VOICE OF CALEB, his son, done by the actor playing Belize.

THE RECORDED VOICE OF ORRIN, his other son, done by the actor playing the Angel.

THE MOTHER, played by the actor playing the Angel.

EMILY, a nurse, played by the actor playing the Angel.

The Continental Principalities, inconceivably powerful Apparatchik/Bureaucrat Aggregate Angelic Entities of whom the Angel of America is a peer:

THE ANGEL EUROPA, played by the actor playing Joe.

THE ANGEL AFRICANII, played by the actor playing Harper.

THE ANGEL OCEANIA, played by the actor playing Belize.

THE ANGEL ASIATICA, played by the actor playing Hannah.

THE ANGEL AUSTRALIA, played by the actor playing Louis.

THE ANGEL ANTARCTICA, played by the actor playing Roy.

The voice at the top of Act One, Scene 1, announcing Prelapsarianov; the recorded greeting in the Mormon Visitors' Center in Act Three, Scene 3; the voice introducing the Council of Principalities in Act Five, Scene 5; and the voice of the BBC reporter in the same scene should be the voice of the actor playing the Angel.

* The character Roy M. Cohn is based on the late Roy M. Cohn (1927–1986), who was all too real; for the most part the acts attributed to the character Roy, such as his illegal conferences with Judge Kaufmann during the trial of Ethel Rosenberg, are to be found in the historical record. But this Roy is a work of dramatic fiction; his words are my invention, and liberties have been taken.

Perestroika *is dedicated to Kimberly T. Flynn*

Because the soul is progressive, it never quite repeats itself, but in every act attempts the production of a new and fairer whole.

—Ralph Waldo Emerson, "On Art"

ACT ONE:

Spooj

December 1985

Scene 1

In the darkness a Voice announces:

A VOICE: In the Hall of Deputies, the Kremlin. December 1985.
Aleksii Antedilluvianovich Prelapsarianov, the World's
Oldest Living Bolshevik.

> *(Lights up on Prelapsarianov at a podium before a great red
> flag. He is unimaginably old and totally blind.)*

ALEKSII ANTEDILLUVIANOVICH PRELAPSARIANOV: The Great
Question before us is: Are we doomed? The Great Question before us is: Will the Past release us? The Great
Question before us is: Can we Change? In Time? And
we all desire that Change will come.
> *(A little pause, then with sudden, violent passion:)*

I

And *Theory*? How are we to proceed without *Theory*? What System of Thought have these Reformers to present to this mad swirling planetary disorganization, to the Inevident Welter of fact, event, phenomenon, calamity? Do they have, as we did, a beautiful Theory, as bold, as Grand, as comprehensive a construct? You can't imagine, when we first read the Classic Texts, when in the dark vexed night of our ignorance and terror the seed-words sprouted and shoved incomprehension aside, when the incredible bloody vegetable struggle up and through into Red Blooming gave us Praxis, True Praxis, True Theory married to Actual Life . . . You who live in this Sour Little Age cannot imagine the grandeur of the prospect we gazed upon: like standing atop the highest peak in the mighty Caucasus, and viewing in one all-knowing glance the mountainous, granite order of creation. We were one with the Sidereal Pulse then, in the blood in our heads we heard the tick of the Infinite. You cannot imagine it. I weep for you.

And what have you to offer now, children of this Theory? What have you to offer in its place? *(Blistering contempt)* Market Incentives? American Cheeseburgers? Watered-down Bukharinite stopgap makeshift Capitalism! NEPmen! Pygmy children of a gigantic race!

Change? Yes, we must must change, only show me the Theory, and I will be at the barricades, show me the book of the next Beautiful Theory, and I promise you these blind eyes will see again, just to read it, to devour that text. Show me the words that will reorder the world, or else *keep silent*.

If the snake sheds his skin before a new skin is ready, naked he will be in the world, prey to the forces of chaos.

Without his skin he will be dismantled, lose coherence and die. Have you, my little serpents, a new skin?

(An immense, booming command) Then we dare not, we *cannot*, we MUST NOT move ahead!

Scene 2

The same night as the end of Millennium Approaches. *Joe and Louis enter Louis's new apartment in the arctic wastes of Alphabetland; barren of furniture, unpainted, messy, grim.*

Tense little pause. Louis embarrassed takes in the room, and begins to gather up the books, newspapers and clothing strewn on the floor, tossing them behind the bed, talking all the while:

LOUIS: Alphabetland. This is where the Jews lived when they first arrived. And now, a hundred years later, the place to which their more seriously fucked-up grandchildren repair. *(Yiddish accent)* This is progress?

(Giving up the housecleaning) It's a terrible mess.

JOE: It's a little dirty.

LOUIS *(Defensive)*: *Messy*, not dirty. That's an important distinction. It's dust, not dirt, chemical-slash-mineral, not organic, not like microbes, more like—

(He walks toward Joe) Can I take your tie off?

JOE *(Stepping back)*: No, wait, I'm, um, um, uncomfortable, actually.

LOUIS: Me, too, actually. Being uncomfortable turns me on.

JOE: Your, uh, boyfriend. He's sick. And I . . .

LOUIS: Very. He's not my boyfriend, we—

3

We can cap everything that leaks in latex, we can smear our bodies with nonoxynol-9, safe, chemical sex. Messy, but not dirty.

(Little pause)

Look I want to but I don't want to beg.

JOE: No, I—

LOUIS: Oh come on. *Please.*

JOE: I should go.

LOUIS: Fine! Ohblahdee, ohblahdah, life goes on. Rah.

JOE: What?

LOUIS: Hurry home to the missus.

(Points to Joe's left-hand ring finger)

Married gentlemen before cruising the Ramble should first remove their bands of gold.

(Joe stares at his wedding ring.)

LOUIS: Go if you're going. Go.

(Joe starts to leave, hesitates, then turns back; he hesitates again, then goes to Louis and hugs him, awkwardly, collegially.)

JOE: I'm not staying.

LOUIS *(Sniffing)*: What kind of cologne is that?

JOE *(A beat, then)*: Fabergé.

LOUIS: OH! *Very* butch, very heterosexual high school. Fabergé.

(Louis gently breaks the hug, steps back a little.)

LOUIS: You smell nice.

JOE: So do you.

LOUIS: Smell is . . . an incredibly complex and underappreciated physical phenomenon. Inextricably bound up with sex.

JOE: I . . . didn't know that.

LOUIS: It is. The nose is really a sexual organ.

Smelling. Is desiring. We have five senses, but only two that go beyond the boundaries . . . of ourselves. When you look at someone, it's just bouncing light, or when you hear them, it's just sound waves, vibrating air, or touch is just nerve endings tingling. Know what a smell is?

JOE: It's . . . some sort of . . . No.

LOUIS: It's made of the molecules of what you're smelling. Some part of you, where you meet the air, is airborne.

(Louis steps carefully closer to Joe, who still seems ready, though not as ready, to bolt.)

LOUIS: Little molecules of Joe . . . *(Leaning in, inhaling deeply)* Up my nose.

Mmmm . . . Nice. Try it.

JOE: Try . . . ?

LOUIS: Inhale.

(Joe leans toward Louis, inhales.)

LOUIS: Nice?

JOE: Yes.

I should—

LOUIS *(Quietly)*: Sssssshhhh.

Smelling. And tasting.

(Moving in closer) First the nose, then the tongue.

JOE *(Taking a half-step back, scared)*: I just don't—

LOUIS *(Stepping forward)*: They work as a team, see. The nose tells the body—the heart, the mind, the fingers the cock—what it wants, and then the tongue explores, finding out what's edible, what isn't, what's most mineral,

5

food for the blood, food for the bones, and therefore most delectable.

(Louis licks the side of Joe's cheek.)

LOUIS: Salt.

(Louis kisses Joe, who holds back a moment and then responds.)

LOUIS: Mmm. Iron. Clay.

(Louis slips his hand down the front of Joe's pants, groping him. Joe shudders. Louis pulls his hand out, smells and tastes his fingers, and then holds them for Joe to smell.)

LOUIS: Chlorine. Copper. Earth.

(They kiss again.)

LOUIS: What does that taste like?
JOE: Um . . .
LOUIS: What?
JOE: Well . . . Nighttime.
LOUIS: Stay?
JOE: Yes.

(They kiss again. Louis starts unbuttoning Joe's shirt.)

JOE: Louis?
LOUIS: Hmmm?
JOE: What did that mean, ohblahdee ohblah—
LOUIS: Sssssh. Words are the worst things. Breathe. Smell.
JOE: But—
LOUIS: Or if you have to talk, talk dirty.

Scene 3

The same night. The sounds of wind and snow. Mr. Lies sits alone, still in his snowsuit, playing the oboe, in what's left of Harper's imaginary Antarctica, which is now bare, grim and grimy.
Mr. Lies stops playing.

MR. LIES: The oboe: official instrument of the International Order of Travel Agents. If the duck was a songbird it would sing like this. Nasal, desolate, the call of migratory things.

(Harper enters dragging a small pine tree which she has felled, its slender stump-end shredded and splintered. The fantasy explorer gear from Act Three, Scene 3, of Millennium *is gone; she is dressed in the hastily assembled outfit in which she fled the apartment at the end of Act Two, Scene 9: a thin pullover, a skirt, torn tights, gloves. She's been outdoors for three days now and looks it—filthy and disheveled. Her previous pioneer determination, stretched thin, has become desperate and angry.)*

HARPER: I'm FREEZING!
MR. LIES *(Pointing to the tree)*: Where did you get that?
HARPER: From the great Antarctic pine forests. Right over that hill.
MR. LIES: There are no pine forests in Antarctica.
HARPER: I chewed this pine tree down. With my teeth. Like a beaver. I'm *hungry*, I haven't eaten in three days! I'm going to use it to build . . . something, maybe a fire.

(She takes a soggy box of matches from under her pullover. She strikes match after match; all dead.

She gives up, and sits on the tree, heavy with despair.)

HARPER: I don't understand why I'm not dead. When your heart breaks, you should die. But there's still the rest of you. There's your breasts, and your genitals, and they're amazingly stupid, like babies or faithful dogs, they don't get it, they just want him. Want him.

(Joe enters the scene, dressed in his Temple garment, barefoot. He looks around, uncertain of where he is till he sees Harper.)

MR. LIES: The Eskimo is back.

HARPER: I know.

I wanted a real Eskimo, someone chilly and reliable, not this, this is just . . . some lawyer, just—

JOE: Hey, buddy.

HARPER: Hey.

JOE: I looked for you. I've been everywhere.

HARPER: Well, you found me.

JOE: No, I . . . I'm not looking now. I guess I'm having an adventure.

HARPER: Can I come with you? This isn't working anymore. I'm cold.

JOE: I wouldn't want you to see.

HARPER: Think it's worse than what I imagine? It's not.

JOE: I should go.

HARPER: Bastard. You fell out of love with me.

JOE: That isn't true, Harper.

HARPER: Why did you come here? Leave me alone if you're so goddamned happy.

JOE: You want me here.

(She nods.)

HARPER: To see you again. Any way I can.
OH GOD I WISH YOU WERE— No I don't.
JOE: Please don't.
HARPER: DEAD.
Come back.

(Little pause.)

JOE: Oh, buddy, I wish so much that I could. But how can I? I can't.

(He vanishes.
Mr. Lies plays the oboe—a brief, wild lament. The magic Antarctic night fades away, replaced by a harsh sodium light and the ordinary sounds of the park and the city in the distance.)

MR. LIES: Blues for the death of Heaven.
HARPER *(Shattered, scared)*: No . . .
MR. LIES: I tried to tell you. There are no Eskimo in Antarctica.
HARPER: No. No trees either.
MR. LIES *(Pointing to the chewed-down pine tree)*: So where did you get that?
HARPER: From the Botanical Gardens Arboretum. It's right over there. Prospect Park. We're still in Brooklyn I guess.

(The lights of a police car begin to flash.)

MR. LIES *(Vanishing)*: The Law for real.
HARPER *(Raising her hands over her head)*: Busted. Damn.
What a lousy vacation.

Scene 4

The same night. In the Pitt apartment in Brooklyn. A telephone rings. Hannah, carrying the bags and wearing the coat she had on in Act Three, Scene 4, of Millennium Approaches, *enters the apartment, drops the bags, and runs for the phone.*

HANNAH *(Exhausted, grim)*: Pitt residence.

No, he's out. This is his mother. No I have no idea where he is. I have no idea. He was supposed to meet me at the airport, but I don't wait more than three and three-quarters—

I— Yes of course I know her, yes she lives here, what's—

OH MY LORD! Is she— Wait, Officer, I don't— She did *what*, exactly?

Why on earth would she chew down a pine tree?

(Severe) You have no business laughing about it, you can stop that right now. That's ugly.

Apology accepted.

I don't know where that is, I just arrived from Salt Lake and I barely found Brooklyn, I had to give the superintendent money to let me into the— I'll take a . . . a taxicab.

No! No hospital! She's not insane, she's just . . . bewildered, she—I don't see how it's any business of yours what she is.

Tell her Mother Pitt is coming.

(Hannah hangs up.)

Scene 5

The same night. Prior in his bedroom, alone, asleep in his bed. The room is intact, no trace of the demolished ceiling. Prior is having a nightmare. He wakes up, frightened.

PRIOR: OH! *(He looks around)* Oh.
> *(He looks under the covers. He discovers that the lap of his pajamas is soaked in cum)*
> Will you look at this!
> First goddamn orgasm in months and I slept through it.

(He dials a number on his bedside telephone.
> *At Belize's workstation on the tenth floor of New York Hospital, a phone rings. Belize, in a colorful version of scrubs [his design and execution], is busy with paperwork.*
> *Prior, while waiting for Belize to answer, grabs a box of Kleenex and, reaching under the covers, blots himself dry.*
> *Belize answers.)*

BELIZE: Ten East.
PRIOR: I am drenched in spooj.
BELIZE *(Continuing to work)*: Spooj?
PRIOR: Cum. Jiz. Ejaculate. I've had a wet dream.
BELIZE: Uh-huh, bound to happen, you've been abstemious to excess: Beaucoup de spooj.
PRIOR: It was a woman.
BELIZE *(Stops working)*: A woman.
PRIOR: Not a *conventional* woman.
BELIZE: Grace Jones.

(Prior looks at the ceiling.)

BELIZE: Hello?

PRIOR: An angel.

BELIZE: Oh FABULOUS.

PRIOR: I feel . . . lascivious. Come over.

BELIZE: I spent the whole day with you, I *do* have a life of my own, you know.

PRIOR: I'm sad.

BELIZE: I thought you were lascivious.

PRIOR: Lascivious sad. Wonderful and horrible all at once, like . . . like there's a war inside. My eyes are funny, I . . . *(He touches his eyes)* Oh.

I'm crying.

BELIZE: Prior?

PRIOR: I'm scared. And also full of, I don't know, Joy or something.

(In the hospital, Henry, Roy's doctor, enters.)

PRIOR: Hope.

HENRY: Are you the duty nurse?

BELIZE *(To Henry)*: Yo.

(To Prior) Look, baby, I have to go—

PRIOR: Oh no, not yet, I— Sing something first. Sing with me.

BELIZE *(To Prior)*: Wash up and sleep and—

HENRY *(Over the line above)*: Are you the duty nurse?

BELIZE *(To Henry)*: *Yo*, I said.

HENRY: Then why are you dressed like that?

BELIZE *(To Henry)*: You don't like it?

(To Prior) I'll call you in the morning when I—

PRIOR: Just one little song. Some hymn?

HENRY: *Nurse. Hang up the fucking—*

BELIZE *(To Henry)*: One moment, *please*. This is an emergency.
   (To Prior, singing:)
      Hark the herald angels sing—

   (Prior joins in:)

PRIOR AND BELIZE:
      Glory to the newborn king.
      Peace on earth and mercy mild,
      God and sinners reconciled—
HENRY *(Over the last line above)*: What's your name?
PRIOR AND BELIZE *(Belize singing louder)*:
      JOYFUL all ye nations rise,
      Join the triumph of the skies!
      With angelic hosts proclaim:
      Christ is born in Bethlehem!
      Hark the herald angels sing,
      Glory to the newborn king!
BELIZE *(To Prior)*: Call you back. There's a man bothering me.
PRIOR: Je t'aime.

   (Belize hangs up. He turns to Henry.)

BELIZE: May I help you?
HENRY: Nurses are supposed to wear white.
BELIZE: Doctors are supposed to be home, in Westchester, asleep.
HENRY: Emergency admit, Room 1013. Here are the charts.

   (He hands medical charts to Belize. Belize scans the chart, reads the patient's name, raises his eyebrows, reads a little more. He looks up at Henry.)

HENRY: Start the drip, Gamma G and he'll need a CTM, radiation in the morning so clear diet and— What?

BELIZE: "Liver cancer."

HENRY: Just— Ignore that, just—

BELIZE: Oncology's on six, doll.

HENRY: This is the right floor.

BELIZE: It says liver can—

HENRY *(Lashing out)*: I don't give a *fuck* what it *says*. *I* said this is the right floor.

BELIZE: Ooooh, testy.

HENRY: He's a very important man.

BELIZE: Then I *shouldn't* fuck up his medication?

HENRY: Think you can manage that? And, maybe, you know, confidentiality, don't share this with your sewing circle.

BELIZE: Safe home.

(Henry leaves.)

BELIZE: Asshole.

(He looks at the chart, shakes his head; after a moment's hesitation he picks up the phone and dials. Prior answers.)

BELIZE: I have some piping hot dish.

PRIOR: How hot can it be at three in the—

BELIZE: Get out your oven mitts. *(Looking around to make sure no one is near, then:)*
    Don't tell anyone, but guess who just checked in with the troubles?
    The Killer Queen Herself. New York's number one closeted queer.

PRIOR: *Koch?*

BELIZE: *No,* not Koch. Better. *(He whispers into the receiver)*

PRIOR: The Lord moves in mysterious ways.

BELIZE: Oh indeed. Indeed She do.

Scene 6

The same night, continuous with Scene 5. Roy in his hospital bed, sick and very scared. Belize enters, putting on latex gloves.

ROY: Get outta here you, I got nothing to say to you.
BELIZE: Just doing my—
ROY: I want a white nurse. My constitutional right.
BELIZE: You're in a hospital, you don't have any constitutional rights.

(Belize begins preparing Roy's right arm for the insertion of an IV drip needle, palpating the vein, disinfecting the skin. He moves to insert the IV needle in Roy's arm.)

ROY *(Nervous)*: Find the vein, you moron, don't start jabbing that goddamned spigot in my arm till you find the fucking vein or I'll sue you so bad they'll repossess your teeth you dim black motherf—
BELIZE *(Had enough; very fierce)*: Watch. Yourself.
     You don't talk that way to me when I'm holding something this sharp. Or I might slip and stick it in your heart. If you have a heart.
ROY: Oh I do. Tough little muscle.
BELIZE: I bet.
     Now I've been doing drips a long time. I can slip this in so easy you'll think you were born with it. Or I can make it feel like I just hooked you up to a bag of Liquid Drano. So you be nice to me or you're going to be one sorry asshole come morning.
ROY: Nice.
BELIZE: Nice and quiet.

(Belize puts the drip needle, painlessly, in Roy's arm. Roy's impressed, but doesn't show it.)

BELIZE: There.

ROY *(Fierce)*: I *hurt.*

BELIZE: I'll get you a painkiller.

ROY: Will it knock me out?

BELIZE: I sure hope so.

ROY: Then shove it. Pain's . . . nothing, pain's life.

BELIZE: Sing it, baby.

ROY: When they did my facelifts, I made the anesthesiologist use a local. They lifted up my whole face like a dinner napkin and I was wide awake to see it.

BELIZE: Bullshit. No doctor would agree to do that.

ROY: I can get anyone to do anything I want. For instance: Let's be friends. Jews and coloreds, historical liberal coalition, right? My people being the first to sell retail to your people, your people being the first people my people could afford to hire to sweep out the store Saturday mornings, and then we all held hands and rode the bus to Selma. Not me of course, I don't ride buses, I take cabs. But the thing about the American Negro is, he never went Communist. Loser Jews did. But you people had Jesus so the reds never got to you. I admire that.

BELIZE: Your chart didn't mention that you're delusional.

ROY: Barking mad. Sit. Talk.

BELIZE: Mr. Cohn. I'd rather suck the pus out of an abscess. I'd rather drink a subway toilet. I'd rather chew off my tongue and spit it in your leathery face. So thanks for the offer of conversation, but I'd rather not.

(Belize starts to exit, turning off the light as he does.)

ROY: Oh forchristsake. Whatta I gotta do? Beg? I don't want to be alone.

(Belize stops.)

ROY: Oh how I fucking *hate* hospitals, nurses, this waste of time and . . . wasting and weakness, I want to kill the—
'Course they can't kill this, can they?

(Belize says nothing.)

ROY: No. It's too simple. It knows itself. It's harder to kill something if it knows what it is. Like pubic lice. You ever have pubic lice?
BELIZE: That is none of your—
ROY: I got some kind of super crabs from some kid once, it took twenty drenchings of Kwell and finally shaving to get rid of the little bastards. *Nothing* could kill them. And every time I had to itch I'd smile, because I learned to respect them, these unkillable crabs, because . . . I learned to identify. You know? Determined lowlife. Like me.
   You've seen lots of guys with this.

(Little pause.)

BELIZE: Lots.
ROY: How do I look, comparatively?
BELIZE: I'd say you're in trouble.
ROY: I'm going to die. Soon.
   That was a question.
BELIZE: Probably. Probably so.
ROY: Hah.

I appreciate the . . . the honesty, or whatever . . .

If I live I could sue you for emotional distress, the whole hospital, but . . .

I'm not prejudiced, I'm not a prejudiced man.

(Belize just looks at him.)

ROY: These racist guys, simpletons, I never had any use for them—too rigid. You want to keep your eye on where the most powerful enemy really is. I save my hate for what counts.

BELIZE: Well. And I think that's a good idea, a good thing to do, probably.

(Little pause. Then, with great effort and distaste:)

This didn't come from me and I *don't* like you but let me tell you a thing or two:

They have you down for radiation tomorrow for the sarcoma lesions, and you don't want to let them do that, because radiation will kill the T-cells and you don't have any you can afford to lose. So tell the doctor no thanks for the radiation. He won't want to listen. Persuade him. Or he'll kill you.

ROY: You're just a fucking nurse. Why should I listen to you over my very qualified, very expensive WASP doctor?

BELIZE: He's not queer. I am.

(Belize winks at Roy.)

ROY: Don't wink at me.

You said "a thing or two." So that's one.

BELIZE: I don't know what strings you pulled to get in on the azidothymidine trials.

ROY: I have my little ways.

BELIZE: Uh-huh.

Watch out for the double blind. They'll want you to sign something that says they can give you M&Ms instead of the real drug. You'll die, but they'll get the kind of statistics they can publish in the *New England Journal of Medicine*. And you can't sue 'cause you signed. And if you don't sign, no pills. So if you have any strings left, pull them, because everyone's put through the double blind and with this, time's against you, you can't fuck around with placebos.

ROY: You hate me.

BELIZE: Yes.

ROY: Why are you telling me this?

BELIZE: I wish I knew.

(Pause.)

ROY *(Very nasty)*: You're a butterfingers spook faggot nurse. I think . . . you have little reason to want to help me.

BELIZE: Consider it solidarity. One faggot to another.

(Belize snaps, turns, exits. Roy calls after him:)

ROY: Any more of your lip, boy, and you'll be flipping Big Macs in East Hell before tomorrow night!

(He picks up his bedside phone)

And get me a real phone, with a hold button, I mean look at this, it's just one little line, now how am I supposed to perform basic bodily functions on *this*?

(He lifts the receiver, clicks the hang-up button several times)

Yeah who is this, the operator? Give me an outside line. Well then dial for me. It's a medical emergency, darling, dial the fucking number or I'll strangle myself with the phone cord.

202-733-8525.

(Little pause)

Martin Heller. Oh hi, Martin. Yeah I know what time it is, I couldn't sleep, I'm busy dying. Listen, Martin, this drug they got me on, azido-methatalo-molamoca-whatchamacallit. Yeah. AZT.

I want my own private stash, Martin. Of serious Honest-Abe medicine. That I control, here in the room with me. No placebos, I'm no good at tests, Martin, I'd rather cheat. So send me my pills with a get-well bouquet, *PRONTO*, or I'll ring up CBS and sing Mike Wallace a song: *(Sotto voce, with relish)* "The Ballad of Adorable Ollie North and His Secret Contra Slush Fund."

(He holds the phone away from his ear; Martin is screaming)

Oh you only *think* you know all I know. *I* don't even know what all I know. Half the time I just make it up, and it *still* turns out to be true! We learned that trick in the fifties. Tomorrow, you two-bit scumsucking shitheel flypaper insignificant dried-out little turd. A nice big box of drugs for Uncle Roy. Or there'll be seven different kinds of hell to pay. *(He slams the receiver down)*

ACT TWO:

The Anti-Migratory Epistle

(For Sigrid)

January 1986

Scene 1

Three weeks after the end of Act One. Prior and Belize stand outside a dilapidated funeral parlor on the Lower East Side. They've just left the funeral of a mutual friend, a major New York City drag-and-style queen. Belize is in defiantly bright and beautiful clothing. Prior is dressed oddly, a long black coat over black shirt and pants, and a large, fringed, black scarf draped like a hood around his head, capped off with black sunglasses; the effect is disconcerting, vaguely suggesting adherence to a severe, albeit elegant, religious discipline.

    Belize has been deeply moved by the service they've just

attended. Prior is closed off in some place as dark as the costume he's wearing.

PRIOR: It was tacky.
BELIZE: It was divine.
He was one of the Great Glitter Queens. He couldn't be buried like a *civilian*. Trailing sequins and incense he came into the world, trailing sequins and incense he departed it. And good for him!
PRIOR: I thought the twenty professional Sicilian mourners were a bit much.
A great queen; big fucking deal. That ludicrous spectacle in there, just a parody of the funeral of someone who *really* counted. We don't; faggots; we're just a bad dream the real world is having, and the real world's waking up. And he's *dead*.

(Little pause.)

BELIZE *(Concerned, irritated)*: Lately, sugar, you have gotten very strange. Lighten up already.
PRIOR: Oh I *apologize*, it was only a for-God's-sake funeral, a cause for fucking *celebration*, sorry if I can't join in with the rest of you death-junkies, gloating about your survival in the face of that . . . of his ugly demise because unlike you I have nothing to gloat about. Never mind.

(Angry little pause.)

BELIZE: And you *look* like Morticia Addams.
PRIOR: Like the Wrath of God.
BELIZE: Yes.

PRIOR: That is the intended effect.

My eyes are fucked-up.

BELIZE: Fucked-up how?

PRIOR: Everything's . . . closing in. Weirdness on the periphery.

BELIZE: Since when?

PRIOR: For three weeks. Since the night when— *(He stops himself)*

BELIZE: Well what does the eye doctor say?

PRIOR: I haven't been.

BELIZE: Oh for God's sake. *Why?*

PRIOR: I was improving. Before.

Remember my wet dream.

BELIZE: The angel?

PRIOR: It wasn't a dream.

BELIZE: 'Course it was.

PRIOR: No. I don't think so. I think it really happened.

I'm a prophet.

BELIZE: Say what?

PRIOR: I've been given a prophecy. A Book. Not a *physical* book, or there was one but They took it back, but somehow there's still this Book. In me. A prophecy. It . . . really happened, I'm—almost completely sure of it.

(He looks at Belize)

Oh stop looking so . . .

BELIZE: You're scaring me.

PRIOR: It was after Louis left me. Every night I'd been having these horrible vivid dreams. And then . . .

(Little pause.)

BELIZE: Then . . . ?

PRIOR: And then She arrived.

Scene 2

Three weeks earlier. The Angel and Prior in Prior's bedroom. The wrecked ceiling, Prior in bed, the Angel in the air.

As the scene shifts, Prior changes out of his prophet garb and into his pajamas onstage. He does this quietly, deliberately, forcing himself back into memory, preparing to tell Belize his tale.

At first, Belize watches from the street, but soon he's drawn into the bedroom.

ANGEL: Greetings, Prophet!
The Great Work Begins:
The Messenger has arrived.
PRIOR *(Terrified)*: Go away.
ANGEL: Attend:
PRIOR *(Still terrified)*: Oh God there's a thing in the air, a thing, a thing.
ANGEL: I I I I
Am the Bird of America, the Bald Eagle,
Continental Principality,
LUMEN PHOSPHOR FLUOR CANDLE!
I unfold my leaves, Bright steel,
In salutation open sharp before you:
Prior WALTER
Long-descended, well-prepared.
PRIOR *(Even more terrified)*: No, I'm not prepared, for anything, I have lots to do, I—
ANGEL *(With a gust of music)*: American Prophet tonight you become,
American Eye that pierceth Dark,
American Heart all Hot for Truth,

The True Great Vocalist, the Knowing Mind,
Tongue-of-the-Land, Seer-Head!

PRIOR: Oh, shoo! You're scaring the shit out me, get the fuck
out of my room. Please, oh please—

ANGEL: Now:

Remove from their hiding place the Sacred Prophetic
Implements.

(Little pause.)

PRIOR: The *what?*

ANGEL: Remove from their hiding place the Sacred Prophetic
Implements.

(Little pause)

Your dreams have revealed them to you.

PRIOR: What dreams?

ANGEL: You have had dreams revealing to you—

PRIOR: I haven't had a dream I can remember in months.

ANGEL *(Stern)*: No . . . *dreams*, you— Are you sure?

PRIOR: Yes. Well, the two dead Priors, they—

ANGEL: No not the heralds, not them. Other dreams.

Implements, you must have—

One moment.

PRIOR: *This*, this is a dream, obviously, I'm sick and so I—well
OK it's a pretty spectacular dream but still it's just some—

ANGEL *(A flash of anger)*: Quiet. Prophet. A moment, please,
I— *(Looking up, addressing unseen forces; severe)* The disorganization is—

(She coughs, looks up, rises higher in the air)

Yes.

(To Prior) In the kitchen. Under the tiles under the sink.

PRIOR: You want me to, to tear up the kitchen floor?

ANGEL: Get a shovel or an axe or some . . . *tool* for dislodging tile and, and grout and unearth the Sacred Implements.

PRIOR: No fucking way! The ceiling's bad enough, I'll lose the lease, I'll lose my security deposit, I'll wake up the downstairs neighbors, their hysterical dog, I—

Do it yourself.

ANGEL *(A tremendous, unearthly voice)*: SUBMIT, SUBMIT TO THE WILL OF HEAVEN!

(An enormous gust of wind knocks Prior over. He glares at her from the floor and shakes his head no. A standoff. The Angel coughs a little. There is a small explosion in the kitchen offstage. A cloud of plaster dust drifts in.)

PRIOR: What did you— What . . . ? *(Exits into the kitchen)*

ANGEL: And Lo, the Prophet was led by his nightly dreams to the hiding place of the Sacred Implements, and— Revision in the text: the Angel helped him to unearth them, for he was weak of body *(Pissed-off)* though not of will.

(Prior returns with an ancient leather suitcase, very dusty.)

PRIOR: You cracked the refrigerator, you probably released a whole cloud of fluorocarbons, that's bad for the, the environment.

ANGEL: My wrath is as fearsome as my countenance is splendid. Open the suitcase.

(Prior does. He reaches inside and produces a pair of bronze spectacles with rocks instead of lenses.)

PRIOR: Oh, look at this.

Like, wow, man, totally Paleozoic. *(He puts them on)*
This is—
(He stops suddenly. His head jerks up. He is seeing something)
OH! OH GOD NO! OH— *(Horror-stricken, he rips off the spectacles)*
That was terrible! I don't want to see that!

ANGEL: Remove the Book.

(Prior removes a large Book with bright steel pages from the suitcase. There is a really glorious burst of music, more light, more wind.)

ANGEL: From the Council of Continental Principalities
Met in this time of Crisis and Confusion:
Heaven here reaches down to disaster
And in touching you touches all of Earth.

(Music. She points to the spectacles.)

ANGEL: Peepstones.

(Prior retrieves them. He's understandably reluctant to put them on.)

ANGEL: Open me Prophet. I I I I am
The Book.
Read.

(Prior starts to put on the peepstones and then stops.)

PRIOR: Wait. Wait.
How come . . . How come I have this, um, erection?
It's very hard to concentrate.

ANGEL: The stiffening of your penis is of no consequence.
PRIOR: Well maybe not to you but—
ANGEL: READ!

(More music, more light. Prior puts the glasses on, and reads.)

ANGEL: You are Mere Flesh. I I I I am Utter Flesh,
    Density of Desire, the Gravity of Skin:
    What makes the Engine of Creation Run?
    Not Physics but Ecstatics Makes the Engine Run:
    (Continue below:)

(She begins to glow with intense sexual heat.)

PRIOR *(Hit by a wave of intense sexual feeling)*: Hmmmm . . .
ANGEL *(Continuous from above)*: The Pulse, the Pull, the Throb,
    the Ooze . . . *(Continue below:)*
PRIOR: Wait, please, I . . . Excuse me for just a minute, just a
minute.
    OK I . . .
ANGEL *(Continuous from above)*: Priapsis, Dilation,
    Engorgement, Flow:
    The Universe Aflame with Angelic Ejaculate . . .
    (Continue below:)
PRIOR *(Losing control, he starts to hump the Book)*: Oh shit . . .
ANGEL *(Continuous from above)*: The Heavens a-thrum to the
    Seraphic Rut,
    The Fiery Grapplings . . . *(Continue below:)*
PRIOR: Oh God, I . . .
ANGEL *(Continuous from above)*: The Feathery Joinings of the
    Higher Orders,
    Infinite, Unceasing, the Blood-Pump of Creation!

(With a rough gesture, she causes Prior to flip over on his back. She's directly above and parallel to him, close.)

PRIOR: OH! OH! I . . .   ANGEL: HOLY Estrus! HOLY
OH! Oh! Oh . . . oh . . .   Orifice!
                          Ecstasis in Excelsis!
                          AMEN!

(Pause. The peepstones have fallen off, or he removes them.)

PRIOR: Oh. Oh God.
ANGEL: The Body is the Garden of the Soul.
PRIOR: What *was* that?
ANGEL: Plasma Orgasmata.
PRIOR: Yeah well no doubt.
BELIZE *(He's heard enough; stepping into the bedroom)*: Whoa whoa whoa wait a minute excuse me please. You fucked this angel?
PRIOR: She fucked me. She has . . . Well, She has eight vaginas.
ANGEL: REGINA VAGINA!
     Hermaphroditically Equipped as well with a Bouquet of Phallī.
     I I I I am Your Released Female Essence Ascendant!
BELIZE: The sexual politics of this are—
PRIOR: Very confusing. I know.

(As Belize challenges Prior, the Angel, unthreatened, intrigued, lands and listens closely.
     From the moment Belize enters the bedroom, Prior is simultaneously with him, on the street, three weeks hence, trying to tell what happened, and present in the bedroom with the Angel, where he's very frightened, with no idea of what's about to happen.)

BELIZE: What . . . So what, um, *gender* is God? According to—

PRIOR: According to Her: male. God is a—

BELIZE: No shit? Seriously? You don't think that's sorta sexist or—

PRIOR: He's not an old man or anything, He's a—from what I gather He's a Hebrew letter.

ANGEL: THE ALEPH GLYPH.

PRIOR: A . . . *male* Hebrew letter.

ANGEL: Deus Erectus! Pater Omnipotens!

PRIOR *(To Belize)*: Each Angel is an infinite aggregate myriad entity, They're basically incredibly powerful bureaucrats, They have no imagination, They can *do* anything but They can't invent, create, They're sort of fabulous and dull all at once, and They copulate, *ceaselessly*, apparently, the Angels, They—I mean I—

BELIZE: They get fucked by a Hebrew letter.

ANGEL *(To Prior)*: READ ON.

(Prior gestures to the Angel to wait.)

PRIOR: When Angels cum They make something called, um— *(Continue below:)*

ANGEL: Plasma orgasmata!

PRIOR *(Continuous from above)*: —plasma orgasmata which makes some . . . other thing called— *(Continue below:)*

ANGEL: Protomatter.

PRIOR *(Continuous from above)*: —protomatter. Right. Which is what makes . . . Everything else.

ANGEL: Creation.

PRIOR: Creation. Heaven's, like, a lot, um, livelier than we were led to—

ANGEL: Heaven Is a City Much Like San Francisco.

(Prior puts on the peepstones and returns to the floor, read-
ing at first from the Book, and then, as the Angel continues,
he stops reading, removes the peepstones and listens to her.
Belize is also listening, watching, bewildered and increas-
ingly scared by the way Prior's sounding.)

ANGEL: House upon house depended from Hillside,
　　　　From Crest down to Dockside,
　　　　The green Mirroring Bay.
　　　　Oh Joyful in the Buckled Garden,
　　　　Undulant Landscape over which
　　　　The Threat of Seismic Catastrophe hangs:
　　　　More beautiful because imperiled.
　　　　POTENT: yet DORMANT: The Fault Lines of
　　　　　　Creation!
　　　　(Coughs)
　　　　When *He*, ALEPH,
　　　　GLYPH From Whom All Words Descend,
　　　　Tearing Glyph from Auto-Generative All-Adoring
　　　　　　Gaze,
　　　　He Would Come Down to Us ABLAZE!
　　　　THEN: Heaven's Walls would Ring with the
　　　　Glad mad moaning of the Winged Throng.
　　　　Hot Wet FIRE would flood the Cosmos,
　　　　And Igneous Gases Enflame the Voids,
　　　　And lights revolve, and spheres resolve,
　　　　As ALEPH Burns.
　　　　He burns . . . forever, He . . .

(A deep sorrow wells up. She can't speak. Little pause. Prior
looks at her.)

31

PRIOR *(Quietly, to the Angel)*: He what?

BELIZE *(To Prior)*: Let's go over to your place . . . *(Continue below:)*

ANGEL: And then . . . *(Pause)* HE . . . CHANGED.

PRIOR *(Over Angel, to Belize)*: No I don't like it there, it's—

BELIZE *(Continuous from above)*: —make some tea and talk about—

(A far-off, deep rumbling.)

PRIOR *(To the Angel, hearing something in her story that's recognizable)*: He changed.
BELIZE *(To Prior)*: God?

(Prior nods.)

BELIZE: Changed how, honey? If He's God, how can He—
PRIOR: I don't know. But He did. He—
ANGEL: He grew weary of Us.
    Our Songs and Fornications.
    His Angels: Who cannot Imagine, who lack that Faculty.
    Made for His Pleasure, We can only ADORE.
    Seeking something New,
    He split the World starkly in Two
    (A mounting fury directed at Prior:)
    And made YOU—
PRIOR *(To Belize)*: When God made people He created . . . division.
ANGEL: Human Beings:
    Uni-Genitalled: Female. Male.

PRIOR *(To Belize)*: He awakened a potential in the design for change—

ANGEL: In creating *You*—

PRIOR *(To Belize)*: —for random event.

ANGEL: Our Father-Lover Unleashed
Eternal Creation's Potential for Change.

PRIOR *(To Belize)*: For movement forward.

ANGEL *(Bitter disgust, envy)*: In *YOU* the Virus of TIME began!
YOU *Think*. And You *IMAGINE*!
Migrate! Explore—

BELIZE: Uh-huh, but . . .

ANGEL: And when you do:

BELIZE: But so like you know none of this is, um, *real*, right?

ANGEL: Paradise itself Shivers and Splits—

PRIOR *(To Belize)*: I, I didn't say it was real, I said it was what She told me, and She's, well . . .

ANGEL: Each Day when *You* Awake—

PRIOR: Real *enough*, I guess, I don't know!

ANGEL *(Her fury now directed at Prior and Belize)*: As though
WE are only
The dream of *YOU*.

PRIOR: Everything's come unglued, right? So is . . . *(The room, the world) this* any less plausible than you know than—

(A low but powerful tremor stops Prior. The Angel hears it, too; Belize doesn't, but he sees Prior hearing it.)

ANGEL *(With loathing)*: PROGRESS!

BELIZE *(To Prior)*: We're not supposed to *migrate*? To progress?

(Another tremor, louder and more powerful.)

ANGEL *(Again, with loathing)*:   PRIOR *(To Belize)*: No, but,
MOVEMENT!   but there are *consequences!*
ANGEL *(Furious, with deep sorrow breaking through)*: Shaking
 HIM!
PRIOR *(To Belize)*: When we move around, heedless of, of—
 When the human race began to travel, intermingle, then—

(A much bigger, nearer, rolling tremor begins and builds. Belize hears it, or imagines that he hears something.)

PRIOR *(To Belize)*: There began to be tremors in Heaven. Earth-
 quakes or, or rather—
BELIZE *(To Prior)*: Intermingle?
PRIOR: Heavenquakes.
BELIZE: Are you hearing yourself?

(Another deep, rolling tremor. All three look up.)

ANGEL: He . . . *began to*—! HE who never was begun, was
 always *IS* and
 Unbegun! He . . . *began* to
 Leave Us!
 Bored with His Angels, *Bewitched* by Humanity, in
 Mortifying Imitation of You, His least creation,
 He would sail off on Voyages, no knowing where.
 Quake follows quake, Absence follows Absence:
 Nasty Chastity and Disorganization; Loss of
 Libido; Protomatter Shortfall . . .

(A huge tremor.)

ANGEL: UH. OH.
 Then:

PRIOR *(To Belize)*: April 18, 1906.

ANGEL: In that day:

PRIOR: It's the Great San Francisco Earthquake.

ANGEL: *In That Day*:
    Father-Lover of the Million Unutterable Names,
    Deus Erectus, Pater Omnipotens, King of the Universe:
    He left—

PRIOR: He. Abandoned Them.

ANGEL: —And did not return.
    We do not know where He has gone.
    He may *never* . . .
    And bitter, cast-off, We wait, bewildered;
    Our finest houses, our sweetest vineyards,
    Made drear and barren, missing Him.

(She coughs. There's a pause, then:)

BELIZE *(To Prior)*: Abandoned.
    I smell a motif.

(Prior looks at Belize, then nods.)

PRIOR: Well it occurred to me.

BELIZE: The man that got away?
    And I think the time has come to let him go.

(Little pause.)

PRIOR *(To Belize, forlorn)*: And then?
    (To the Angel) And then what?

ANGEL: Surely you see towards what We are Progressing:

(Prior goes back to the Book. He takes up the peepstones but doesn't put them on.)

35

ANGEL: The fabric of the sky unravels:
>   Angels hover, anxious fingers worry the tattered edge.
>   Before the boiling of blood and the searing of skin
>   comes the Secret catastrophe:
>   Before Life on Earth becomes finally merely impossible,
>   It will for a long time before have become completely
>   unbearable.
>   *(Coughs, then, with great passion and force:)*
>   *YOU HAVE DRIVEN HIM AWAY!* YOU MUST
>   STOP MOVING!

PRIOR *(Quiet, frightened)*: Stop moving.

ANGEL *(Softly, rapidly)*: Forsake the Open Road: Neither Mix
>   Nor Intermarry
>   Let Deep Roots Grow: If you do not MINGLE you
>   will Cease to Progress. Seek Not to Fathom the
>   World and its Delicate Particle Logic: You cannot
>   Understand, You can only Destroy, You Do not
>   "Advance," You only Trample.
>   Poor blind Children, abandoned on the Earth,
>   Groping terrified, misguided, over
>   Fields of Slaughter, over bodies of the Slain:
>   HOBBLE YOURSELVES!
>   There is No Zion Save Where You Are!
>   If you Cannot find your Heart's desire—

PRIOR: —In your own backyard—

ANGEL, PRIOR AND BELIZE: You never lost it to begin with.

(The Angel coughs. Prior is disturbed and confused by the citation; she is confused and disturbed that humans know these lines. For Belize it's proof, of course, that this is a dream.)

ANGEL: Turn Back.

PRIOR: Please, please, whatever you are, angel or, or—

ANGEL: Undo.

PRIOR: I'm not a prophet, I'm a sick, lonely man, I—

ANGEL: Till He—

PRIOR: I don't . . . *understand* this visitation—

ANGEL: Till HE returns again.

(The Angel picks up the Book. Prior is now both terrified and very angry.)

PRIOR: Stop moving. That's what you want. Answer me! You want me dead.

(Pause. The Angel and Prior look at one another.)

PRIOR: Uh-huh, well *I. I'M TIRED!* Tired to death of, of being done to, um, *infected*, fucked-over and tortured by, by you, by this—

Is this, is this, disease, is the virus in me, is that the, the epistle, is that the prophecy? Is this just . . . *revenge*, because we, because you think we ruined . . .

No. No, I want you to go away, you go away or *I* will, I'll leave, I can leave, too, I'll—

(The Angel steps aside and gestures to Prior to leave. He hesitates and starts for the door. As he passes near her, the Angel touches him gently on the shoulder.)

ANGEL *(Leaning in, quiet, intimate)*: You can't Outrun your Occupation, Jonah. Hiding from Me one place you will find me in another.

(She takes her hand from his shoulder.)

ANGEL: I I I I stop down the road, waiting for you.

(Tenderly, she puts her arm about his waist.)

ANGEL *(Almost a whisper)*: You Know Me Prophet: Your
      battered heart,
      Bleeding Life in the Universe of Wounds.

(The Angel presses the Book against Prior's chest, then presses her body against his. Together they experience something unnameable—painful, joyful, in equal measure. There is a terrible sound.)

ANGEL: Vessel of the BOOK now: Oh Exemplum Paralyticum:
      On you in you in your blood we write have written:
      STASIS!
      The END.

(She releases Prior, who sinks to the floor. In gales of music, holding the Book aloft, the Angel ascends.)

Scene 3

The bedroom disappears. While this is happening, Prior stands, and, again, with deliberate, unhurried pace, changes into his street clothes. When he's ready he resumes his place beside Belize, who's waiting, thinking, on the street in front of the funeral home.

    Prior and Belize stare at one another, silent for a beat, and then:

BELIZE: Uh-huh. I . . .
      Well what do you want me to say?

PRIOR: It's . . . nuts.

BELIZE: It's . . . *worse* than nuts, it's— "Don't migrate"? "Don't mingle"? That's . . . kind of malevolent, isn't it, 'cause— *(Continue below:)*

PRIOR: I hardly think it's appropriate for you to get *offended*, I didn't invent this shit it was *visited* on—

BELIZE *(Continuous from above)*: —you know, some of us didn't exactly *choose* to migrate, know what I'm saying, some of us— But it *is* offensive or at least monumentally confused and it's not . . . *visited*, Prior. By who? It *is* from you, what else is it?

PRIOR: Something else.

BELIZE: That's crazy.

PRIOR: Then I'm crazy.

BELIZE: No, you're—

PRIOR: Then it was an angel.

BELIZE: It was *not* an—

PRIOR: Then I'm crazy. The whole world is, why not me? It's 1986 and there's a *plague*, friends younger than me are dead, and I'm only thirty, and every goddamn morning I wake up and I think Louis is next to me in the bed and it takes me long minutes to remember . . . that this is *real*, it isn't just an impossible, terrible dream, so maybe yes I'm flipping out.

BELIZE *(Angry)*: Stop.

(Tough, harsh, very clear) This is not dementia. And this is not real. This is just you, Prior, afraid of . . . Of what's coming. Afraid of time.

But see that's just not how it goes, the world doesn't spin backwards.

(Prior starts to say something. Belize holds up his hand, forbidding, and Prior obeys.)

BELIZE: Listen to the world, to how fast it goes.

(They listen, and the sounds of the city grow louder and louder, filling the stage, sounds of traffic, whistles, alarms, people, all very fast and very complex and very determinedly moving ahead.)

BELIZE: That's New York traffic, baby, that's the sound of energy, the sound of time. Even if you're hurting, it can't go back.

You better fucking not flip out. There's no angel. You hear me? For me? *(Continue below:)*

THE ANGEL'S VOICE: Whisper into the ear of the World, Prophet. *(Continue below:)*

BELIZE *(Continuous from above)*: I can handle anything but not this happening to you.

THE ANGEL'S VOICE *(Continuous from above)*: Wash up red in the tide of its dreams,

And billow bloody words into the sky of sleep.

(Prior steps back from Belize, withdrawing.)

PRIOR: I'm sorry, baby, I . . . I've tried, really, but . . . I can't, it follows me, it won't let me go. So, maybe I'm a prophet. Not me, alone, all of us, the, the ones who're dying now. Maybe the virus is the prophecy? Be still. Maybe the world has driven God from Heaven. Because, because I do believe that, that over and over, I've seen the end of things. And *(He puts his hand near his eyes)* having seen, I'm going blind, as prophets do. Right? It makes a certain sense to me.

THE ANGEL'S VOICE: FOR THIS AGE OF ANOMIE: A NEW LAW! *(Continue below:)*

PRIOR: Oh, *oh God* how I hate Heaven. But I've got no resistance left.

THE ANGEL'S VOICE *(Continuous from above)*: Delivered this
    night, this silent night, from Heaven,
    Oh Prophet, to You.

(Prior kisses Belize good-bye.)

PRIOR: Except to run.

(He limps away. Belize watches him go.)

ACT THREE:

Borborygmi

(The Squirming Facts Exceed the Squamous Mind)

January 1986

Scene 1

Several days after the end of Act Two. Split scene: Joe and Louis in bed in Louis's apartment, which is tidier, homier. Louis is sound asleep. Joe is awake, sitting up, watching Harper, who is in the living room of their Brooklyn apartment. She's dressed in a soiled nightgown. Returning Joe's stare, she removes her nightgown; she stands shivering, facing him in her bra, panties and stockings.

Hannah, in a bathrobe, enters the Brooklyn living room, carrying a dress over her arm and a pair of shoes. She puts the shoes down in front of Harper.

HANNAH: Good you're out of that nightdress, it was starting to smell.

HARPER: You're telling me.

43

HANNAH: Now let's slip this on.

(They put the dress on Harper.)

HANNAH: Good.
HARPER: I hate it.
HANNAH: It's pretty.
    Shoes?

(Harper steps into them.)

HANNAH: Now let's see about the hair.

(Harper bends over; Hannah combs Harper's hair.)

HANNAH: It can be very hard to accept how disappointing life is, Harper, because that's what it is, and you have to accept it. With faith and time and hard work you reach a point where . . . where the disappointment doesn't hurt as much, and then it gets easy to live with. Quite easy. Which . . . is in its own way a disappointment. But. There.
HARPER: In my old life, my previous life, I never used to get up at five A.M.
    (To Joe) This is a nightmare.
HANNAH: I said I'd open up.
HARPER *(Fake admiration)*: You volunteered.
HANNAH: I can't sit around, idle.
HARPER: You just got here, you could . . . sightsee, you could—
HANNAH: I didn't come for fun.
HARPER: You came to the right place.
HANNAH: I leave messages for him at work. They say he's not in but I know he is, but he won't take my calls. He's ashamed.

JOE: She's right.
HANNAH: I'll fix myself.
JOE: I am.
HANNAH: And we can go.

(Hannah exits.)

HARPER: You're in love with him.

(She crosses into Louis's bedroom. Joe shrinks from her, afraid, but he's careful not to wake Louis.)

JOE: I am?
HARPER: Don't ask *me*. Are you?
JOE: How're you doing?
HARPER: Huh. Maybe you're not in love with him. If you were, you wouldn't ask me that. You wouldn't be brave enough. You'd know.
LOUIS *(Still asleep, starting to wake)*: Joe . . . ?
JOE: Yeah, yeah, screwy   HARPER: Talk softer you're
stomach, nothing.   waking him up.

(Louis is asleep again.)

HARPER: I have terrible powers. Maybe I'm a witch.
JOE: You're not a—
HARPER: I see more than I want to see. You can't do that. I could be a witch. Why not? I married a fairy. Anything's possible, any awful thing.
JOE: Leave, Harper.
HARPER: I knew you'd be with someone. You think of yourself as so lonely all the time, but you've never been alone.
JOE: Oh that isn't . . . You don't know. I have felt very alone.

HARPER: Till now.

(Harper puts her hand under Louis's head, and pushes up; Louis startles awake.)

LOUIS: Who are you . . . ?
JOE *(To Louis)*: I— It's nothing, just . . .
    (To Harper) Go.

(She vanishes.)

JOE *(To Louis)*: Morning.
    Sleep well?
LOUIS: No.
    Did you?
JOE: Soundly.
LOUIS: How do you manage that? These fucking dreams, every . . .
    Don't you have—
JOE: I don't dream.
LOUIS: Everybody dreams.
JOE: I don't.
LOUIS: *Ever?*
JOE: Not that I can remember.
    Not since I started, um, being here, with you.
LOUIS *(A beat, then)*: You're a conundrum.
JOE: Solve me.
    (Embarrassed) Sorry, that was really—
LOUIS: But you can't—
JOE: Weird, that was really—
LOUIS: You can't *solve* conundrums, they're . . . bafflements, you can only, um . . .
JOE: Conjecture.

(Louis nods.)

JOE: So ask me something.

LOUIS: Like . . . ?

JOE: Something you've never asked me before.
It should be easy, you haven't asked much.

(Louis looks around the room, as if not recognizing any of it, then he stares hard at Joe. A beat, then:)

LOUIS: Who *are* you?

Scene 2

Same day. Roy in his hospital room; near his bed, there's a mini-fridge with a locked door. He looks worse than before, gaunt, gray. The pain in his gut is now constant and it's getting worse. He's on the phone, a more elaborate model than the one in the previous scene; this phone has buttons.

ROY: No records no records what are you deaf I said I have no records for their shitty little committee, it's not how I work I—

(He has a severe abdominal spasm. He holds the phone away, grimaces terribly, curls up into a ball and then uncurls, making no sound, determined that the party on the line won't hear how much pain he's in.

Ethel Rosenberg appears in her hat and coat. Roy sees her enter. He watches her walk to a chair and sit. He resumes his phone call, never taking his eyes off Ethel, who stares at him, silent, unreadable.)

ROY: Those notes were lost. LOST. In a fire, water damage, I can't do this any—

(Belize enters with a pill tray.)

ROY *(To Belize)*: I threw up fifteen times today! I *COUNTED*.
(To Ethel) What are *you* looking at?
(To Belize) Fifteen times. *(He goes back to the phone)* Yeah?

BELIZE: Hang up the phone, I have to watch you take these—

ROY: The LIMO thing? Oh for the love of Christ I was acquitted twice for that, they're trying to kill me dead with this *harassment*, I have done things in my life but I never killed anyone.
(To Ethel) Present company excepted. And you *deserved* it.
(To Belize) Get the fuck outta here.
(Back to the phone) Stall. It can't start tomorrow if we don't show, so don't show, I'll pay the old harridan back. I have to have a—

BELIZE: Put down the phone.

ROY: Suck my dick, Mother Teresa, this is life and death.

BELIZE: Put down the—

(Roy grabs the pill cup off the tray and throws the pills on the floor. Belize reaches for the phone. Roy slams down the receiver and snatches the phone away, protecting it, cradling it.)

ROY: You touch this phone and I'll bite. And I got rabies.
And from now on, I supply my own pills. I already told 'em to push their jujubes to the losers down the hall.

BELIZE: Your own pills.

ROY: No double blind. A little bird warned me. The vultures are—

(Another severe spasm. This time he makes noise)

Jesus God these cramps, now I know why women go beserk once a— AH FUCK!

(He has another spasm. Ethel laughs.)

ROY: Oh good I made her laugh.

(The pain is slightly less. He's a little calmer)

I don't trust this hospital. For all I know Lillian fucking *Hellman* is down in the basement switching the pills around. No, wait, she's dead, isn't she? Oh boy, memory, it's— Hey, Ethel, didn't Lillian die, did you see her up there, ugly, ugly broad, nose like a . . . like even a Jew should worry mit a punim like that. You seen somebody fitting that description up there in Red Heaven? Hah?

(To Belize) She won't talk to me. She thinks she's some sort of a deathwatch or something.

BELIZE: Who are you talking to?

(Roy looks at Ethel, realizing/remembering that Belize can't see her.)

ROY: I'm self-medicating.

BELIZE: With what?

ROY *(Trying to remember)*: Acid something.

BELIZE: Azidothymedine?

ROY: Gesundheit.

(Roy retrieves a key on a ring from under his pillow and tosses it to Belize.)

BELIZE: AZT? You got . . . ?

(Belize unlocks the ice box; it's full of bottles of pills.)

ROY: One-hundred-proof elixir vitae.

Give me the key.

BELIZE: You scored.

ROY: Impressively.

BELIZE: Lifetime supply.

There are maybe thirty people in the whole country who are getting this drug.

ROY: Now there are thirty-one.

BELIZE: There are a hundred thousand people who need it.

Look at you. The dragon atop the golden horde. It's not fair, is it?

ROY: No, but as Jimmy Carter said, neither is life. And then we shipped him back to his peanut plantation. Put your brown eyes back in your goddamn head, baby, it's the history of the world, I didn't write it, though I flatter myself I am a footnote. And you are a nurse, so minister and skedaddle.

BELIZE: If you live fifty more years you won't swallow all these pills.

(Pause)

I want some.

ROY: That's illegal.

BELIZE: Ten bottles.

ROY: I'm gonna report you.

BELIZE: There's a nursing shortage. I'm in a union. I'm real scared.

I have friends who need them. Bad.

ROY: Loyalty I admire. But no.

BELIZE *(Amazed, off-guard)*: *Why?*

(Pause.)

ROY: Because you repulse me. *"WHY?"* You'll be begging for it next. *"WHY?"* Because I hate your guts, and your friends' guts, that's *why.* "Gimme!" So goddamned entitled. Such a shock when the bill comes due.

BELIZE: From what I read you never paid a fucking bill in your life.

ROY: *No one* has worked harder than me. To end up knocked flat in a—

BELIZE: Yeah well things are tough all over.

ROY: And you come *here* looking for *fairness? (To Ethel)* They couldn't *touch* me when I was alive, and now when I'm dying they try this: *(He grabs up all the paperwork in two fists)* Now! When I'm a— *(He can't find the word. Back to Belize)* That's fair? What am I? A dead man!

(A terrible spasm, quick and violent; he doubles up. Then, when the pain's subsided:)

Fuck! What was I saying Oh God I can't remember any . . . Oh yeah, dead.

I'm a goddamn dead man.

BELIZE: You expect *pity?*

ROY *(A beat, then)*: I expect you to hand over that key and move your nigger ass out of my room.

BELIZE: What did you say?

ROY: Move your nigger cunt spade faggot lackey ass out of my room.

BELIZE *(Overlapping, starting on "spade")*: Shit-for-brains filthy-mouthed selfish motherfucking cowardly cocksucking cloven-hoofed pig.

ROY *(Overlapping, starting on "cowardly")*: Mongrel. Dinge. Slave. Ape.

BELIZE: Kike.

ROY: *Now* you're talking!

BELIZE: Greedy kike.

ROY: Now you can have a bottle. But only one.

(Belize tosses the key at Roy, hard. Roy catches it. Belize takes a bottle of the pills, then another, then a third, and then leaves.
As soon as Belize is out of the room Roy is spasmed with pain he's been holding in.)

ROY: GOD! *(The pain subsides a little)* I thought he'd never go! *(It subsides a little more. Then to Ethel)* So what? Are you going to sit there all night?

ETHEL: Till morning.

ROY: Uh-huh. The cock crows, you go back to the swamp.

ETHEL: No. I take the 7:05 to Yonkers.

ROY: What the fuck's in Yonkers?

ETHEL: The disbarment committee hearings. You been hocking about it all week. I'll have a look-see.

ROY: They won't let you in the front door. You're a convicted and executed traitor.

ETHEL: I'll walk through a wall.

(She laughs. He joins her.)

ROY: Fucking SUCCUBUS!

(They're laughing, enjoying this.)

ROY: Fucking blood-sucking old bat!

(They continue to laugh as Roy picks up the phone, punches a couple of buttons and then stops dialing, his laughter gone. He stares at the phone, dejectedly, not noticing that Ethel has vanished.
Roy puts the receiver back in its cradle and puts the phone aside. He turns to the empty chair where Ethel had been sitting. He talks to the chair as if she's sitting in it.)

ROY: The worst thing about being sick in America, Ethel, is you are booted out of the parade. Americans have no use for sick. Look at Reagan: he's so healthy he's hardly human, he's a hundred if he's a day, he takes a slug in his chest and two days later he's out west riding ponies in his PJs. I mean *who does that?* That's America. It's just no country for the infirm.

Scene 3

Same day. The Diorama Room of the Mormon Visitors' Center. The room's a small proscenium theater; the diorama is hidden behind closed red velvet curtains. There are plush red theater seats for the audience, and Harper is slouched in one of them, dressed as she was in her previous scene. Empty potato chip and M&M bags and cans of soda are scattered around her seat. She stares with dull anger at the drawn stage curtains. She's been here a long time.
     Hannah enters with Prior, dressed in his prophet garb.

HANNAH: This is the Diorama Room.
     (To Harper) I thought we agreed that you weren't—
     (To Prior) I'll go see if I can get it started.

(She exits. Prior sits. He removes his scarf and dark glasses. He wipes his face, startlingly pale and clammy with sweat, with the scarf. He breathes in and out, feeling tightness in his lungs.
     Harper watches this with a level stare and a flat affect— jaded, ironic disaffection she's self-protectively, experimentally assumed.
     The lights in the room dim. After a blare of feedback/static, a Voice on tape [the Angel's] intones:)

53

A VOICE: Welcome to the Mormon Visitors' Center Diorama Room. In a moment, our show will begin. We hope it will have a special message for you. Please refrain from smoking, and food and drink are not allowed. *(A chiming tone)* Welcome to the Mormon Visitors'—

(The tape lurches into very high speed, then smears into incomprehensibly low speed, then stops, mid-message, with a loud metallic blat, which frightens Prior. The lights remain dim.)

HARPER: They're having trouble with the machinery.

(She rips open a bag of M&Ms and offers them to Prior.)

PRIOR: No thanks, I—
    You're not supposed to eat in the—
HARPER: I can. I live here. Have we met before?
PRIOR: No, I don't . . . think so. You *live* here?
HARPER: There's a dummy family in the diorama, you'll see when the curtain opens. The main dummy, the big daddy dummy, looks like my husband, Joe. When they push the buttons he'll start to talk. You can't believe a word he says but the sound of him is reassuring. It's an *incredible* resemblance.
PRIOR: Are you a Mormon?
HARPER: Jack Mormon.
PRIOR: I beg your pardon?
HARPER: Jack Mormon. It means I'm flawed. Inferior Mormon product. Probably comes from jack rabbit, you know, I *ran*.
PRIOR: Do you believe in angels? In the Angel Mormon?
HARPER: Moroni, not Mormon, The Angel Moroni. Ask my mother-in-law, when you leave, the scary lady at the

reception desk: If its name was Moroni why don't they call themselves Morons. It's from comments like that you can tell I'm jack. You're not a Mormon.

PRIOR: No, I—

HARPER: Just . . . distracted with grief.

PRIOR *(Startled)*: I'm not. I was just walking and—

HARPER: We get a lot of distracted, grief-stricken people here. It's our specialty.

PRIOR: I'm not . . . distracted, I'm doing research.

HARPER: On Mormons?

PRIOR: On . . . angels. I'm a . . . an angelologist.

HARPER: I never met an angelologist before.

PRIOR: It's an obscure discipline.

HARPER: I can imagine. Angelology. The field work must be rigorous. You'd have to drop dead before you saw your first specimen.

PRIOR *(A beat, then deciding to confide)*: One . . . I saw one. An angel. It crashed through my bedroom ceiling.

HARPER: Huh. That sort of thing always happens to me.

PRIOR: I have a fever. I should be in bed but I'm too anxious to lie in bed.

You look *very* familiar.

HARPER: So do you. But—

But it's just not possible. I don't get out. I've only ever been here, or in some place a lot like this, alone, in the dark, waiting for the dummy.

(Dramatic music as the house lights dim in the Diorama Room, the red curtains part and stage lights come up to reveal a brightly painted, brightly lit backdrop of the desert between Colorado and Utah, mountains looming in the distance. Posed before the backdrop, in silhouette, a family of Mormon pioneers, seated in a covered wagon.)

A VOICE: In 1847, across fifteen hundred miles of frontier wilderness, braving mountain blizzards, desert storms, and renegade Indians, the first Mormon wagon trains made their difficult way towards the Kingdom of God.

(During the above, Harper noisily rips open a bag of Nacho-Flavored Doritos, which she holds out to Prior:)

HARPER: Want some Nacho-Flavored—

(She stops as, to the accompaniment of the sounds of a wagon train and the Largo from Dvořák's 9th Symphony, stage lights illuminate the Mormon family of costumed mannequins: two young sons, a mother and a daughter, and, driving the wagon, a father, who looks a lot like Joe.)

HARPER *(To the Mormon father)*: Hi Joe.

(The music and background sounds give way as the diorama scene begins. When either Caleb or Orrin speaks, his immobile face is hit with a pinspot; this has an unintentionally eerie effect. The father's face is animated, but not his body.)

CALEB *(Voice on tape)*: Father, I'm a-feard.
FATHER: Hush, Caleb.
ORRIN *(Voice on tape)*: The wilderness is so vast.
FATHER: Orrin, Caleb, hush. Be brave for your mother and your little sister.

CALEB: We'll try, Father, we want you to be proud of us. We want to be brave and strong like you.
ORRIN: When will we arrive in

HARPER: They don't have any lines, the sister and the mother. And only his face moves. That's not really fair.

Zion, Father? When will our
great exodus finally be done?
All this wandering . . .
FATHER: Soon, boys, soon, just
like the Prophet promised.
The Lord leads the way.
CALEB: Will there be lots to eat
there, Father? Will the desert
flow with milk and honey?
Will there be water there?
FATHER: The Lord will provide
for us, Son, he always has.
ORRIN: Well, not *always* . . .
FATHER: Sometimes He tests
us, Son, that's His way, but—
CALEB: Read to us, Father,
read us the story!
FATHER *(Chuckles)*: *Again?*
CALEB AND ORRIN: Yes! Yes!
The story! The story! The
story about the Prophet!
FATHER: Well, boys, well:

1823, the Prophet, who was a
strapping lad, like everyone else
in his time, was seeking God,
there were many churches,
disputatious enough, but who was
Right? Could only be One True
Church. All else darkness—

HARPER *(After "Zion")*:
Never. You'll die of snake
bite and your brother looks
like scorpion food to me!
PRIOR: Sssshhhhh!

HARPER: No. Just sand.
(After "water") Oh, there's a
big lake but it's *salt*, that's
the joke, they drag you on
your knees through hell
and when you get there
the water of course is
undrinkable. Salt.

It's a Promised Land,
but *what* a disappointing
promise!

(After the first "story")
The story! The story!
The story about the
Prophet!

*(Louis suddenly appears in the diorama. The lights onstage
and in the dark auditorium shift, subtly.)*

57

LOUIS: OK yeah yeah yeah but then answer me this: How can a fundamentalist theocratic religion function participatorily in a pluralist secular democracy? I can't *believe* you're a Mormon! I can't believe I've spent two whole weeks in bed with a Mormon!

JOE: Um, could you talk a little softer, I—

LOUIS: Are you busy?

JOE: I'm working, but— And it's closer to three weeks, almost, it's—

LOUIS: But you're a lawyer! A *serious* lawyer!

PRIOR *(Frightened)*: Oh my God, oh my God. What— *what is going on here?*

JOE: The Chief Clerk of the Chief Justice of the Supreme Court is a Mormon, Louis.

HARPER: You know him?

LOUIS: He *is?*

PRIOR *(Closing his eyes)*: I'm delirious, I must be delirious.

(Joe nods yes.)

LOUIS: Jesus, Mormons everywhere, it's like *Invasion of the Body Snatchers.* I don't like cults.

JOE: The Church of Jesus Christ of Latter Day Saints is not a cult.

LOUIS: Any religion that's not at least two thousand years old is a cult. And I know people who would call *that* generous.

JOE: Are you upset about anything?

LOUIS: Oh, you, you noticed? Yeah, I'm . . . *(Continue below:)*

PRIOR: WHAT IS HE DOING IN THERE?

(Joe gets down from the wagon and goes to Louis.)

HARPER: Who? The little creep? He's in and out every day. I hate him. He's got absolutely *nothing* to do with the story.

LOUIS *(Continuous from above)*: I am, I'm upset about, about . . . *(He starts to cry, then stops himself)* You . . . unsettle me. You . . . abandoned your wife, and that's terrible, but you're not a terrible person, and yet you seem so unbothered by what you did, and that's terrible, too, but you're so decent and openly kind and truly sweet in bed, and I don't see how that's possible, but with you it seems to be, so, so . . . *(Continue below:)*

PRIOR *(Standing, grabbing his things in a panic; to Harper)*: Can you turn it off? The . . . I'm leaving, I can't . . .

LOUIS *(Continuous from above)*: Is it just that, you know, belonging to a political party that's one half religious-zealot-control-freak theocrats and one half ego-anarchist-libertarian cowboys, you've had a lot of practice straddling cognitive dissonance? Or, or what?

I can't . . .

(Joe kisses Louis.

Prior starts to leave, but the pain in his leg stops him; he's too weak to run. He turns back to the diorama, and calls:)

PRIOR: Louis!

LOUIS *(Hearing him)*: Did you . . .

JOE: What?

LOUIS: Sssshh! I, I thought I heard . . .

(To himself) Fucking hell.

(To Joe) We have to talk.

JOE: I can't leave the office in the middle of the—

LOUIS: Fuck work! This is a, a crisis. Now.

(Louis exits. Joe follows.)

HARPER *(Alarmed)*: Oh! But the, but he— The dummy never *left* with the little creep, he never *left* before. When they come in and they see he's gone, they'll blame me.

(Harper rushes to the diorama stage and pulls its curtains closed. She turns back and sees that Prior is crying.)

HARPER *(Trying hard to sound hard)*: You shouldn't do that in here, this isn't a place for real feelings, this is just story-time here. *Stop.*

PRIOR: I never imagined losing my mind was going to be such hard work.

HARPER: Oh, it is.

(Her tough veneer starts to crack) Find someplace else to be miserable in. This is *my* place and I don't want you to do that here!

PRIOR: I JUST SAW MY LOVER, MY . . . ex-lover, with a . . . with your husband, with that . . . window-display Ken doll, in that . . . *thing*, I saw him, I—

HARPER: OK OK don't have a hissy fit, I told you it wasn't working right, it's just . . . the magic of the theater or something. Listen, if you see the creep, tell him to bring Joe, to, to bring the mannequin back, they'll evict me and this is it, it's nothing but it's the last place on earth for me. I can't go sit in Brooklyn.

(Hannah enters with a flashlight.)

HANNAH: What on earth is going—
(She sees Prior crying. She glares at Harper)
What did you do to him?

HARPER: Nothing! He just can't *adjust*, is all, he just—

(Hannah goes to the diorama.)

HARPER: NO WAIT, don't—

(Hannah yanks the curtain open. The father dummy is back—a real dummy this time.)

HARPER: Oh. *(To Prior)* Look, we . . . imagined it.

HANNAH: This is a favor, they let me work here as a favor, but you keep making scenes, and look at this mess, it's a garbage scow! *(Continue below:)*

HARPER *(To Prior)*: It doesn't look so much like him, now. He's changed. Again. *(Continue below:)*

HANNAH *(Continuous from above)*: Are you just going to sit here forever, trash piling higher, day after day till—well till what? *(Continue below:)*

HARPER *(Continuous from above, to Hannah)*: You sound just like him. You even grind your teeth in your sleep like him.

HANNAH *(Continuous from above)*: If I could get him to come back I would go back to Salt Lake tomorrow. *(Continue below:)*

HARPER *(Continuous from above)*: You can't go back to Salt Lake, you sold your house! *(Continue below:)*

HANNAH *(Continuous from above)*: But I know my duty when I see it, and if you and Joe could say the same we—

HARPER *(Continuous from above, to Prior)*: My mother-in-law! She sold her house! Her son calls and tells her he's a homo and what does she do? She sells her house! And she calls *me* crazy! *(To Hannah)* You have less of a place in this world than *I* do if that's possible.

PRIOR *(To Harper)*: Am I dreaming this, I don't understand.

HARPER: He saw an angel.

HANNAH: That's his business.

HARPER: He's an angelologist.

ANGELS IN AMERICA

PRIOR: Well don't go blabbing about it.

HANNAH *(Losing the little cool she came in with; to Prior)*: If you aren't serious you shouldn't come in here.

HARPER: Either that or he's nuts.

PRIOR *(To Hannah, also losing it)*: It's a *visitors'* center; I'm *visiting.*

HARPER: He has a point.

HANNAH *(To Harper)*: Quiet!

   (To Prior) It's for serious visitors, it's a serious religion.

PRIOR: Do they like, *pay* you to do this?

HARPER: She volunteers.

PRIOR: Because you're not very hospitable. I did see an angel.

HANNAH *(Blowing up!)*: *And what do you want me to do about it? I have problems of my own.*

   The diorama's closed for repairs. You have to leave.

   (To Harper) Clean up this mess. *(She exits)*

(Harper and Prior look at each other.)

PRIOR: Oh God, I'm exhausted.

HARPER: You don't look well. You really should be home in bed.

PRIOR: I'll die there.

HARPER: Better in bed than on the street. Just ask anyone.

(Prior gathers his things. He looks around the Diorama Room, and then at the trash around Harper's seat, and then at Harper.)

PRIOR: Maybe you should leave, too.

HARPER: I'm waiting.

PRIOR: For what?

(Harper points to the Mormon Mother in the diorama.)

62

HARPER: His wife. His mute wife. I'm waiting for her to speak. Bet her story's not so jolly.

(Prior looks at Harper, afraid. He remembers where they've met.)

PRIOR: Dreaming used to be so . . . safe.

HARPER: It isn't, though, it's dangerous, imagining to excess. It can blow up in your face. Threshold of revelation.

(Prior startles; then, as he searches for something to say:)

HARPER: Till we meet again.

(Prior leaves.
Harper sits alone for a bit, then, addressing the Mormon Mother:)

HARPER: Bitter lady of the Plains, talk to me. Tell me what to do.

(The Mormon Mother turns to Harper, then stands and leaves the diorama stage. She gestures with her head for Harper to follow her.
Harper goes to the diorama, gets in the Mormon Mother's seat.)

HARPER *(To the dummy father)*: Look at us. So perfect in place. The desert the mountains the previous century. Maybe I could have believed in you then. Maybe we should never have moved east.
(To the Mormon Mother) I'm stuck. My heart's an anchor.

MORMON MOTHER: Leave it, then. Can't carry no extra weight.

HARPER: Was it a hard thing, crossing the prairies?

MORMON MOTHER: You ain't stupid. So don't ask stupid. Ask something for real.

HARPER *(A beat, then)*: In your experience of the world. How do people change?

MORMON MOTHER: Well it has something to do with God so it's not very nice.

God splits the skin with a jagged thumbnail from throat to belly and then plunges a huge filthy hand in, he grabs hold of your bloody tubes and they slip to evade his grasp but he squeezes hard, he *insists*, he pulls and pulls till all your innards are yanked out and the pain! We can't even talk about that. And then he stuffs them back, dirty, tangled and torn. It's up to you to do the stitching.

HARPER: And then get up. And walk around.

MORMON MOTHER: Just mangled guts pretending.

HARPER: That's how people change.

(They exit.)

Scene 4

Late that afternoon. Split scene: Joe and Louis at Jones Beach, and later, Prior in his apartment, and Louis at a Brooklyn payphone.

Joe and Louis are sitting shoulder to shoulder in the dunes, facing the ocean. It's cold. The sound of waves and gulls and distant Belt Parkway traffic. New York Romantic. Joe is very cold, Louis as always is oblivious to the weather.

LOUIS: The winter Atlantic. Wow, huh?

There used to be guys in the dunes even when it snowed. Nothing deterred us from the task at hand.

JOE: Which was?

LOUIS: Exploration. Across an unmapped terrain. The body of the homosexual human male. Here, or the Ramble, or the scrub pines on Fire Island, or the St. Mark's Baths. Hardy pioneers. Like your ancestors.

JOE: Not exactly.

LOUIS: And many have perished on the trail.

I fucked around a lot more than he did. No justice.

(Little pause.)

JOE: I love it when you can get to places and see what it used to be. The whole country was like this once. A paradise.

LOUIS: Ruined now.

JOE: It's still a great country. Best place on earth. Best place to be.

LOUIS *(Staring at him a beat, then)*: OY. A *Mormon.*

JOE: You never asked.

LOUIS: So what else haven't you told me?

Joe?

So the fruity underwear you wear, that's . . . ?

JOE: A temple garment.

LOUIS: *Oh my God.* What's it for?

JOE: Protection. A second skin. I can stop wearing it if you—

LOUIS: How can you stop wearing it if it's a skin? Your past, your beliefs, your—

JOE: I know how you feel, I keep expecting Divine Retribution for this, but . . .

I'm actually happy. Actually.

LOUIS: You're not happy, that's ridiculous, no one is happy. What am I doing? With you? With *anyone,* I should be exterminated but with *you*: I mean politically, and, and you're probably bisexual, and, and I mean I really *like* you a lot, but—

(Joe puts his hand over Louis's mouth.)

LOUIS: So, like, *this* is kind of hot . . .
JOE: Shut up, OK?

(Louis nods. Joe takes his hand off Louis's mouth and, after looking all around, kisses him, deeply.)

JOE: You know why you find the world so unsatisfying?

(Louis shakes his head no.)

JOE: Because you believe it's perfectible.
LOUIS: No I—
JOE: You tell yourself you don't, but you do, you cling to fantasies of perfection, and, and kindliness, and you never face the sorrow of the world, its bitterness. The parts of it that are bitter.
LOUIS *(Intrigued)*: Huh.
JOE: You have to reconcile yourself to the world's unperfectibility.
LOUIS *(Nodding)*: Reconcile. And . . . And how do you do that?

(Joe kisses Louis again, begins to unbutton Louis's shirt.)

JOE: By being thoroughly in the world but not of it.
LOUIS: You, you mean like a like an Emersonian kind of kind of thing? I don't see how that's um workable, practical, given, you know, *emotions* and—

(Joe bites Louis's nipple.)

LOUIS: Oh God . . .

JOE: You have to accept that we're not put here to make the entire earth into a heaven, you have to accept we can't. And accept as rightfully yours the happiness that comes your way.

LOUIS: But . . . *Rightfully?* That's . . . so . . . Republican, it's— Bite my nipple again.

(Joe does. Louis responds. Joe starts to unzip Louis's pants. Louis stops him.)

LOUIS: No, wait, fuck, I'm like lost in an ideological leather bar with you. I want my, my *clarity* back, what little I ever possessed, it's been stolen by, I mean, I mean I wish you weren't so, so . . .

JOE: Conservative.

LOUIS: No. So fucking gorgeous. *And conservative!* Though if you were gorgeous and your politics didn't horrifically suck I'd really be in trouble here, but yes, I do sort of wish you weren't responsible for everything bad and evil in the world.

JOE *(Not taking the bait, trying to keep the sex going forward)*: You give me way too much credit.

LOUIS: Right, I mean, Reagan deserves his fair share.

(Joe playfully pulls Louis's hair, but Louis shakes his hand away. Louis's withdrawal is beginning to make Joe apprehensive: something's up.)

JOE: You're obsessed, you know that? If people like you didn't have President Reagan to demonize, where would you be?

LOUIS: If he didn't have people like me to demonize where would *he* be? Upper-right-hand square on *The Hollywood Squares.*

JOE *(Seriously)*: I'm not your enemy. Louis.

LOUIS: I never said you were my—

JOE: Fundamentally, we both want the same thing.

(Little pause. Louis nods his head yes, then:)

LOUIS: I don't think that's true.

JOE: It is.

What you did . . . When you walked out on him, that was, it must've been hard. To do that. The world may not understand it or approve but . . . You did what you needed to do. And, and since I first met you, I . . . I consider you very brave. I don't think I've ever met anyone as—

LOUIS: Nobody does what I did, Joe. Nobody.

JOE: But maybe many want to.

This is so . . . This isn't . . . But.

(Beat)

I. I'm maybe . . . falling in—

(Louis laughs, embarrassed and alarmed.)

LOUIS: No you're not.

JOE *(Angry)*: Don't laugh at— Don't say that. I am. I'm—

LOUIS: You're not! You can't be, it's only been two weeks.

(Continue below:)

JOE: Three, actually, and what difference does that— I've never felt so, um, so happy to, so *hungry* for anyone before, it's like all the time I—

LOUIS *(Continuous from above)*: It takes *years* to . . . feel like that, love, love, ohmygod, *love*, if there even is such a thing as, as— You *think* you do but that's just the, the gay virgin thing, that's—

JOE: You and I, Louis, we're the same. We are. We both want the same thing. We both—

LOUIS: I want to see Prior again.

(Joe freezes, then turns away.)

LOUIS: I miss him, I—

JOE: You want to go back to—

LOUIS: I just . . . need to see him again.

　　It's like a, a bubble rising through rock, it's taken time, these weeks, with you, but—

　　Don't you . . . You must want to see your wife.

(Little pause.)

JOE: I miss her, I feel bad for her, I . . . I'm afraid of her.

LOUIS: Yes.

JOE: And I want more to be with—

LOUIS: I have to. See him.

　　Please don't look so sad.

　　Do you understand what I—

JOE: You don't want to see me anymore.

LOUIS *(Uncertainly)*: I—

JOE: Louis.

　　Anything.

LOUIS: What?

JOE: Anything. Whatever you want. I can give up anything.

　　My skin.

(Joe starts to remove his clothes. When he realizes what Joe is doing, Louis tries to stop him.)

LOUIS: What are you doing, someone will see us, it's not a nude beach, it's freezing!

(Joe pushes Louis away, Louis falls, and Joe removes the rest of his clothing, tearing the temple garment off. He's naked.)

JOE: I'm flayed. No past now. I could give up anything. Maybe . . . in what we've been doing, maybe I'm even infected.

LOUIS: No you're—

JOE: I'm so . . . afraid of that. Of things I never knew I'd ever be afraid of, things I didn't even know existed until we— I'm afraid, now, maybe for the first time, really . . . um, scared.

Because I don't want to be sick. I want to live now. Maybe for the first time ever. And . . .

And I can be anything, anything I need to be. And I want to be with you.

(Louis starts to gather up Joe's clothes and dress him.)

JOE: You have a good heart and you think the good thing is to be guilty and kind always but it's not always kind to be gentle and soft, there's a genuine violence softness and weakness visit on people. You ought to think about that.

LOUIS: I will. Think about it.

JOE: You ought to think about—

LOUIS: Yeah, I will.

JOE: —about what you're doing to me. No, I mean— *(Continue below:)*

LOUIS: I'm sorry, I will, I, I tried to warn you that I—

JOE *(Continuous from above)*: *What you need.* Think about what you need. Be brave.

(Louis starts to walk away from Joe. Joe calls after him:)

JOE: And then you'll come back to me.

(Louis turns back to Joe, then turns again and leaves the beach. Joe starts to dress himself, then sinks to his knees in the sand.

Prior returns home to his apartment. He unwraps his layers of black prophet clothes. He is sweating heavily and feels very sick.

He goes to the sink, runs water, splashes a little on his face, shudders.

Joe, on the beach, looks up and yells:)

JOE: YOU'LL COME BACK TO ME!

(Joe remains, kneeling in the sand, trying to collect himself, unable to move.

Louis is now at a payphone at the edge of a parking lot near the beach.

Prior, in his apartment, takes one pill each from three different bottles, puts them in his mouth, then puts his mouth to the faucet.

Louis dials a number.

In Prior's apartment, the phone rings. Prior's still swallowing. He grabs the phone.)

PRIOR: Wait, I have a mouthful of pills and water, I—
LOUIS: Prior? It's Lou.

(Prior swallows.)

LOUIS: I want to see you.

ACT FOUR:

John Brown's Body

January 1986

Scene 1

Two days later. Roy and Joe in Roy's hospital room. Roy's in a big hospital chair, the kind that makes it possible for very sick people to sit upright briefly. The tube of an IV drip bag, hanging from a portable drip stand, runs into a vein in his arm. He's shockingly altered, in terrible shape. He wears a flimsy hospital bathrobe; under that, a backless hospital johnny gown, and under that, adult diapers. His legs are bare, fish-belly white, and there are disposable hospital slippers on his feet.

He forces himself to speak as normally as he can, using energy he doesn't have, to focus and stay connected.

Joe sits in an ordinary chair, facing Roy.

ROY: If you want the smoke and puffery you can listen to Kissinger and Schultz and those guys, but if you want to look at the heart of modern conservatism, you look at me.

Everyone else has abandoned the struggle, everything nowadays is just sipping tea with Nixon and Mao, that was *disgusting*, did you see that? Were you born yet?

JOE: Of course I—

ROY: My generation, we had *clarity*. Unafraid to look deep into the miasma at the heart of the world, what a pit, what a nightmare is there—*I* have looked, I have searched all my life for absolute bottom, and I found it, *believe* me: *Stygian*. How tragic, how brutal life is. How false people are. The immutable heart of what we are that bleeds through whatever we might become. All else is vanity.

I don't know the world anymore.

(He coughs)

After I die they'll say it was for the money and the headlines. But it was never the money: it's the moxie that counts. I never waivered. You: remember.

JOE: I will, Roy.

(Pause. Roy is sunk in silence. Joe is moved by what Roy's said, but he doesn't know how to respond. He clears his throat, then:)

JOE: I left my wife.

(Little pause)

I needed to tell you.

ROY: It happens.

JOE: I've been staying with someone. Someone else.

ROY: It happens.

JOE: With a . . .

I was afraid you wouldn't want to see me. If you'd forgive me. For letting you down.

ROY *(A shrug)*: I forgive you. But I don't forget. Or I forget but I don't forgive, I can't remember which, what does it—

(Suddenly looking around) You seen a lady around here, dumpy lady, stupid . . . hat? She . . . Oh boy. Oh boy, no she's off watching the hearings. Treacherous bitch.

JOE: Who?

ROY: Did you get a blessing from your father before he died?

JOE: A blessing?

ROY: Yeah.

JOE: No.

ROY: He should have done that. Life. That's what they're supposed to bless. Life.

(Roy motions for Joe to come over, then for him to kneel. Joe hesitates, then kneels.

Roy puts his hand on Joe's forehead. Joe leans the weight of his head into Roy's hand. They both close their eyes and enjoy it for a moment.)

JOE *(Quietly)*: Roy, I . . . I need to talk to you about—

ROY: Ssshah. Schmendrick. Don't fuck up the magic.

(He removes his hand) A *Brokhe*. You don't even have to trick it out of me, like what's his name in the Bible.

JOE: Jacob.

ROY: That's the one. A ruthless motherfucker, some bald runt, but he laid hold of his birthright with his claws and his teeth. Jacob's father—what was the guy's name?

JOE: Isaac.

ROY: Yeah. The sacrifice. That jerk.

My mother read me those stories.

See this scar on my nose? When I was three months old, there was a bony spur, she made them operate, shave it off. They said I was too young for surgery, I'd outgrow it but she insisted. I figure she wanted to toughen me up. And it worked.

I am tough. It's taking a lot . . . to dismantle me.
(He winces; he's having trouble masking the pain he's in)
Now you have to go.

(Joe stands, slowly, reluctant to leave.)

JOE: OK, I— But I.
The person I'm staying with?
It's not a . . .
(Forcing himself to say it) It's a . . . man.

(Pause.)

ROY: A man?
JOE: Yes.

(Little pause.)

ROY: You're with a man?
JOE: Yes I . . .

(He doesn't look at Roy. Roy however is looking hard at him.)

JOE: Yes. I, I guess I am, yes, it's someone I met, recently,
we—for three weeks now, actually, we . . .
(He laughs, embarrassed)
Although I don't know if I, if he wants to, um, continue what . . .
And I'm going kinda crazy, a little, I can't, I don't
know what I'll do if he, if he . . .

(Joe looks at Roy, who is now looking away.)

JOE: I guess it's a surprise to you, that I'm— I hope this is OK. There's no one I can talk to about it, I never wanted to talk about, about this, but now I'm going pillar to post, looking for, for oh Lord I don't know— *(Another laugh, angry, then, putting the word in air quotes)* "Sympathy"? I suppose? Which I never used to need, which I never wanted, never allowed or even, um *felt* for myself, I always found the whole idea of it just contemptible, just . . . repulsive— *(Continue below:)*

ROY *(Very soft, adrift, strange)*: Yeah . . .

JOE *(Not hearing Roy, continuous from above)*: —and I know how . . . preposterous this is, coming at you with this, but you . . .

I know you care for me. I know that. And I'm so—

(Roy starts to stand up.)

ROY: I gotta . . .

JOE: You . . . Oh I'm sorry, I'm— What, the . . . um, bathroom or . . . ?

(Roy walks unsteadily. The IV tube in his arm extends to its full length and then pulls. Roy looks down at it, remembering it's there. In a calm, disinterested manner he pulls it out of his arm, which starts bleeding profusely.)

ROY: Ow.

JOE: Roy, what are you—

(Joe starts for the door. Roy stands still, watching dark blood run down his arm.)

JOE *(Calling off)*: Um, help, please, I think he—

77

(Belize enters with the portable oxygen, and then sees Roy.)

BELIZE: Holy shit.

(Belize puts on rubber gloves, starts toward Roy.)

ROY *(To Belize)*: Get the fuck away from me.
JOE *(Going toward Roy)*: Roy, please, get back into—
ROY *(To Joe)*: SHUT UP!
    Now you listen to me.
BELIZE *(To Roy)*: Get your—
ROY *(To Belize)*: SHUT UP I SAID.
    (To Joe) I want you home. With your wife. Whatever else you got going, cut it dead.
JOE: Oh. Oh I, I *can't*, Roy, I need to be with him, I need to, I'm—

(Roy grabs Joe by the shirt, smearing it with blood.)

ROY: YOU NEED? *Listen to me. You do what I say. Or you will regret it.*

(Roy lets go of Joe's shirt, turning from him, disoriented, looking for the bed.)

ROY *(To Joe)*: And don't talk to me about it. *Ever again.*

(Belize moves in, takes Roy to the bed and begins bandaging the punctured arm.)

ROY *(To Joe)*: I . . . never saw that coming. You kill me.
BELIZE *(To Joe)*: Get somewhere you can take off that shirt and throw it out, and don't touch the blood.
JOE: Why? I don't unders—

ROY: OUT! OUT! You already got my blessing— WHAT MORE DO YOU WANT FROM ME?

(He has a terrible wracking spasm.)

BELIZE *(To Joe)*: Get the fuck outta here!

JOE *(To Roy)*: Please, wait, let me just wait till—

ROY *(Exhausted)*: Till *what*? You what, you want to stay and watch *this*? Well fuck you, too.

(Joe leaves.

Belize finishes bandaging Roy's arm, both of them silent for as long as this takes.

When he's finished with the arm, Belize straightens up a little. Roy looks blankly at the bandage, then:)

ROY: Every goddamn thing I ever wanted they have taken from me. Mocked and reviled, all my life.

BELIZE: Join the club.

ROY: I don't belong to any club you could get through the front door of.

You watch yourself you take too many liberties.

What's your name?

BELIZE *(A beat, then)*: Norman Arriaga. Belize to my friends, but you can call me Norman Arriaga.

ROY: Tell me something, Norman, you ever hire a lawyer?

BELIZE: No Roy. Never did.

ROY: Hire a lawyer, sue somebody, it's good for the soul.

Lawyers are . . . the High Priests of America. We alone know the words that made America. Out of thin air. We alone know how to use The Words. The Law: the only club I ever wanted to belong to. And before they take that from me, I'm going to die.

(Roy has a series of awful spasms, the worst so far; they shake him violently. Roy grabs Belize by both arms. Belize tries to control Roy's body as he convulses in horrible pain. Roy hangs onto Belize; they're in a tight, desperate embrace, both shaken by Roy's agonized spasming.
During this seizure, Ethel appears.)

ROY: Sssshhh. Fire. Out.

(The pain subsiding a little, Roy forces the convulsions to abate. Through the remainder of the scene, with grim effort, conserving his resources, he just manages to keep his body under his control.)

ROY: God have mercy. This is a lousy way to go.
BELIZE: God have mercy.
ROY *(Seeing Ethel)*: Look who's back.
BELIZE *(Looking around, seeing no one)*: Who?
ROY: Mrs. Reddy Kilowatt.
    Fucking horror. How's . . . Yonkers?
BELIZE: I almost feel sorry for you.
ETHEL: A bad idea.
ROY: Yeah. Pity. Repulsive.
    (To Belize) You. Me. *(He snaps his fingers)* No. Connection.
    (Looking at Ethel) Nobody . . . with me now. But the dead.

Scene 2

Same day. Louis sitting alone, cold, on a park bench.
   Prior enters and sits on the bench, as far as he can from Louis.

PRIOR: Oh this is going to be so much worse than I'd imagined.
LOUIS: Hello.
PRIOR: Fuck you you little shitbag.
LOUIS: Don't waste energy beating up on me, OK? I'm already taking care of that.
PRIOR: Don't see any bruises.
LOUIS: Inside.
PRIOR: You are one noble guy. *Inside.* Don't flatter yourself, Louis.
   So. It's your tea party. Talk.
LOUIS: It's good to see you again. I missed you.
PRIOR: Talk.
LOUIS: I want to . . . try to make up.
PRIOR: Make up.
LOUIS: Yes. But—
PRIOR: Aha. But.
LOUIS: But you don't have to be so hostile. Don't I get any points for trying to arrive at a resolution? Maybe what I did isn't forgivable but—
PRIOR: It isn't.
LOUIS: But. I'm trying to be responsible. Prior. There are limits. Boundaries. And you have to be reasonable. *(Unable not to ask) Why are you dressed like that?*
PRIOR *(A challenging, cold smile)*: You were saying something about being reasonable.
LOUIS: I've been giving this a lot of thought. Yes I fucked up, that's obvious. But maybe you fucked up too. You

never trusted me, you never gave me a chance to find my footing, not really, you were so quick to attack and . . . I think, maybe just too much of a victim, finally. Passive. Dependent. And what I think is that people do have a choice about how they handle—

PRIOR *(Cutting to the chase)*: You want to come back. Why? Atonement? Exoneration?

LOUIS: I didn't say I wanted to come back.

(Pause.)

PRIOR: Oh.
    No, you didn't.

LOUIS *(Softly, almost pleading)*: I can't. Move in again, start all over again. I don't think it'd be any different.

(Little pause. Prior looks hard at Louis.)

PRIOR: You're seeing someone else.

LOUIS *(Shocked)*: What? No.

PRIOR: You are.

LOUIS: I'M NOT. Well, occasionally a . . . He's a . . . just a pickup, how do you—

PRIOR: Threshold of revelation. Now: Ask me how I know he's a Mormon.

(Louis stares, shocked; Prior's as surprised as Louis.)

PRIOR: *Is* he a Mormon?
    (Little pause, then impressed and frightened:)
    Well, goddamn.
    Ask me how I knew.

LOUIS: How?

PRIOR *(Furious)*: Fuck you! I'm a prophet!

Reasonable? Limits? Tell it to my *lungs*, stupid, tell it to my lesions, tell it to the cotton-woolly patches in my eyes!

LOUIS: Prior, I . . . haven't seen him for days now, I just—

PRIOR: I'm going, I have limits, too.

(Prior starts to leave. He has an attack of respiratory trouble. He sits heavily on the bench. Louis reaches out to him; Prior waves him away.

Louis cries. Prior looks at Louis.)

PRIOR: You cry, but you endanger nothing in yourself. It's like the idea of crying when you do it. Or the idea of love.

So. Your *boyfriend*—

LOUIS: He's not my—

PRIOR: Tell me where you met him.

LOUIS: In the park. Well, first at work, he—

PRIOR: He's a lawyer or a judge?

LOUIS: Lawyer.

PRIOR: A Gay Mormon Lawyer.

LOUIS: Yes. Republican too.

PRIOR: A Gay Mormon Republican Lawyer. *(With scathing contempt)* Louis . . .

LOUIS: But he's sort of, I don't know if the word would be . . . well, in a way sensitive, and I—

PRIOR: Ah. A *sensitive* gay Republican.

LOUIS: He's just company. Companionship.

(Pause.)

PRIOR: Companionship. Oh.

You know just when I think he couldn't possibly say anything to make it worse, he does. Companionship. How *good*. I wouldn't want you to be *lonely*.

83

There are thousands of gay men in New York City with
AIDS and nearly every one of them is being taken care of
by . . . a friend or by . . . a lover who has stuck by them
through things worse than my . . . So far. Everyone got
that, except me. I got you. Why? What's wrong with me?

(Louis is crying again.)

PRIOR: Louis? Are you really bruised inside?
LOUIS: I can't have this talk anymore.
PRIOR: Oh the *list* of things you can't do. So fragile! Answer
me: Inside: Bruises?
LOUIS: Yes.
PRIOR: Come back to me when they're visible. I want to see
black and blue, Louis, I want to see blood. Because I can't
believe you even *have* blood in your veins till you show
it to me. So don't come near me again, unless you've got
something to show.

(Prior leaves.)

Scene 3

Night of the following day. Roy's hospital room. There are several new machines, monitoring Roy's condition, which is considerably worse. Roy is sleeping a deep, morphine-induced sleep. Belize enters, carrying a tray and a glass of water. With some difficulty he wakes up Roy.

BELIZE: Time to take your pills.

ROY *(Waking, very disoriented)*: What? What time of . . .
Water.

(Belize gives him a glass of water. Roy takes a sip.)

ROY: Bitter.
Look out there. Black midnight.
BELIZE: You want anything?
ROY: Nothing that comes from there. As far as I'm concerned
you can take all that away.
(Seeing Belize) Oh . . .
BELIZE: What?
ROY: Oh. The bogeyman is here.
Lookit, Ma, a schvartze toytenmann.
Come in, sweetheart, what took you so long?
BELIZE: You're flying, Roy. It's the morphine. They put mor-
phine in the drip to stop the . . . You awake? Can you
see who I am?
ROY: Oh yeah, you came for my mama, years ago.
(Confiding, intimate) You wrap your arms around me
now. Squeeze the bloody life from me. OK?
BELIZE: Uh, no, it's not OK. You're stoned, Roy.
ROY: Dark strong arms, take me like that. Deep and sincere but
not too rough, just open me up to the end of me.
BELIZE *(A beat, then gently)*: Who am I, Roy?
ROY: The Negro night nurse, my negation. You've come to
escort me to the underworld. *(A serious sexual invitation)*
Come on.

*(A weight of sadness descends on Belize. He puts down the pill
tray and bends close over Roy:)*

BELIZE: You want me in your bed, Roy? You want me to take
you away.

ROY: I'm ready . . .

BELIZE: I'll be coming for you soon. Everything I want is in the end of you.

(Belize starts to move away from Roy.)

ROY: Let me ask you something, sir.

BELIZE: *Sir?*

ROY: What's it like? After?

BELIZE: After . . . ?

ROY: This misery ends.

BELIZE: Hell or Heaven?

ROY: Aw, come on . . . Jesus Christ, who has time for these . . . games . . .

BELIZE: Like San Francisco.

ROY: A city. Good. I was worried . . . it'd be a garden. I hate that shit.

BELIZE: Mmmm.

Big city, overgrown with weeds, but flowering weeds.

(Roy smiles and nods. Belize sits on the bed, next to Roy.)

BELIZE: On every corner a wrecking crew and something new and crooked going up catty-corner to that. Windows missing in every edifice like broken teeth, fierce gusts of gritty wind, and a gray, high sky full of ravens.

ROY: Isaiah.

BELIZE: Prophet birds, Roy.

Piles of trash, but lapidary like rubies and obsidian, and diamond-colored cow-spit streamers in the wind. And voting booths.

ROY: And a dragon atop a golden horde.

BELIZE: And everyone in Balenciaga gowns with red corsages, and big dance palaces full of music and lights and racial impurity and gender confusion.

(Roy laughs softly, delighted.)

BELIZE: And all the deities are Creole, mulatto, brown as the mouths of rivers.

(Roy laughs again.)

BELIZE: Race, taste and history finally overcome.
    And you ain't there.
ROY *(Shaking his head no in happy agreement)*: And Heaven?
BELIZE *(A beat, then)*: That *was* Heaven, Roy.
ROY: The fuck it was.
    (Suspicious, frightened) Who are you?

(Belize stands up.)

BELIZE *(Soft, calming)*: Your negation.
ROY: Yeah. I know you. Nothing. A stomach grumble that wakes you in the night.

(Ethel enters.)

BELIZE: Been nice talking to you. Go to sleep now, baby. I'm just the shadow on your grave.

Scene 4

The next day. Joe in his office at the courthouse in Brooklyn. He sits dejectedly at his desk. Prior and Belize enter the corridor outside.

PRIOR *(Whisper)*: That's his office.
BELIZE *(Whisper)*: This is stupid.
PRIOR *(Whisper)*: Go home if you're chicken.
BELIZE: *You're* the one who should be home.
PRIOR: I have a hobby now: haunting people. Fuck home. You wait here. I want to meet my replacement.

(Prior goes to Joe's door, opens it, steps in.)

PRIOR: Oh.
JOE: Yes, can I—
PRIOR: You look just like the dummy. She's right.
JOE: Who's right?
PRIOR: Your wife.

(Pause.)

JOE: What?
      Do you know my—
PRIOR: No.
JOE: You said my wife.
PRIOR: No I didn't.
JOE: Yes you did.
PRIOR: You misheard. I'm a Prophet.
JOE: What?
PRIOR: PROPHET PROPHET I PROPHESY I HAVE SIGHT I *SEE*.
      What do *you* do?

JOE: I'm a clerk.

PRIOR: Oh big deal. A clerk. You *what*, you file things? Well you better be keeping a file on the hearts you break, that's all that counts in the end, you'll have bills to pay in the world to come, you and your friend, the Whore of Babylon.

(Little pause)

Sorry wrong room.

(Prior exits, goes to Belize.)

PRIOR *(Despairing)*: He's the Marlboro Man.

BELIZE: Oooh, I wanna see.

(Joe is standing, perplexed, when Belize enters the office. Belize instantly recognizes Joe.)

BELIZE: *Sacred* Heart of Jesus!

JOE: Now what is—

You're Roy's nurse. I recognize you, you're—

BELIZE: No you don't.

JOE: From the hospital. You're Roy Cohn's nurse.

BELIZE: No I'm not. Not a nurse. We all look alike to you. You all look alike to us. It's a mad mad world. Have a nice day.

(Belize exits, runs back to Prior.)

PRIOR: Home on the range?

BELIZE: Chaps and spurs. Now girl we *got* to get you home and into—

PRIOR: Mega-butch. He made me feel beyond nelly. Like little wispy daisies were sprouting out my ears. Little droopy wispy wilted—

(Joe comes out of his office.)

BELIZE: Run! Run!
JOE: Wait!

(They're cornered by Joe. Belize averts his face, masking his mouth and chin with his scarf.)

JOE: What game are you playing, this is a federal courthouse. You said . . . something about my wife. Now what . . . How do you know my—
PRIOR: I'm . . . Nothing. I'm a mental patient. He's my nurse.
BELIZE: Not his nurse, I'm not a n—
PRIOR: We're here because my will is being contested. Um, what is that called, when they challenge your will?
JOE: Competency? But this is an appellate court.
PRIOR: And I am *appealing* to anyone, anyone in the universe, who will listen to me for some . . . Charity . . . Some people are so . . . *greedy*, such pigs, they have everything, health, *everything*, and still they want more.
JOE: You said my wife. And I want to know, is she—
PRIOR: TALK TO HER YOURSELF, BULLWINKLE! WHAT DO I LOOK LIKE A MARRIAGE COUNSELOR?

(To Belize) Oh, nursey dear, fetch the medication, I'm starting to rave.
BELIZE: Pardons, Monsieur l'Avocat, nous sommes absolument Desolée.

(Prior blows a raspberry at Joe.)

BELIZE: Behave yourself, cherie, or nanny will have to use the wooden spoon.

(Prior exits.)

BELIZE *(To Joe, dropping scarf disguise)*: I am trapped in a world of white people. That's *my* problem. *(He exits)*

Scene 5

The next day. At the Bethesda Fountain in Central Park. It's cold, and as the scene progresses a storm front moves in and the sky darkens. Louis is sitting on the fountain's rim. Belize enters and sits next to him.

BELIZE: Nice angel.

LOUIS: What angel?

BELIZE: The fountain.

LOUIS *(Looking)*: Bethesda.

BELIZE: What's she commemorate? Louis, I'll bet you know.

LOUIS: The . . . Croton Aqueduct, I think. Right after the Civil War. Prior loves this—

BELIZE: The Civil War. I knew you'd know.

LOUIS: I know all sorts of things. The sculptress was a lesbian.

BELIZE: Ooh, a sister! That a fact? You are nothing if not well informed.

LOUIS: Listen. I saw Prior yesterday.

BELIZE: Prior is *upset.*

LOUIS: This guy I'm seeing, I'm not seeing him now. Prior misunderstood, he jumped to—

BELIZE: Oh yeah. Your new beau. Prior and me, we went to the courthouse. Scoped him out.

LOUIS: *You had no right to do that.*

BELIZE: Oh did we violate your *rights*. *(Continue below:)*

LOUIS: Yeah, sort of, and, and— Couldn't you have done this on the phone, you needed to, what? Extract every last drop of, of schadenfreude, get off on how unhappy I am, how—

BELIZE *(Continuous from above)*: You walk out on your lover. Days don't pass before you are out on the town with somebody new. But this— *"Schadenfreude"? (Continue below:)*

LOUIS: I'm *not* out on the— I want you to tell Prior that I—

BELIZE *(Continuous from above)*: *This* is a record low: sharing your dank and dirty bed with Roy Cohn's buttboy.

(Pause.)

LOUIS: Come again?

BELIZE: Doesn't that bother you at all?

LOUIS: *Roy Cohn?* What the fuck are you— I am not sharing my bed with Roy Cohn's . . .

BELIZE: Your little friend didn't tell you, huh? You and Hoss Cartwright, it's not a verbal kind of thing, you just kick off your boots and hit the hay.

LOUIS: Joe Pitt is not Roy Cohn's— Joe is a very moral man, he's not even *that* conservative, or, well not that *kind* of a . . . And I don't want to continue this.

BELIZE *(Starting to go)*: Bye-bye.

LOUIS: It's not my fault that Prior left you for me.

BELIZE: I beg your pardon.

LOUIS: You have always hated me. Because you are in love with Prior and you were when I met him and he fell in love with me, and so now you cook up this . . . I mean how do you know this? That Joe and *Roy Cohn* are—

BELIZE: I don't know whether Mr. Cohn has penetrated more than his *spiritual* sphincter. All I'm saying is you better hope there's no GOP germ, Louis, 'cause if there is, you got it.

LOUIS: *I don't believe you.* Not . . . *Roy Cohn.* Joe wouldn't— Not *Roy Cohn.* He's, he's like the polestar of human evil, he's like the worst human being who ever lived, the, the damage he's done, the years and years of, of . . . criminality, that whole era, that— Give me fucking credit for *something*, please, some little moral shred of, of, of *something*, OK sure I fucked up, I fucked up everything, I didn't want to, to face what I needed to face, what life was insisting I face but I don't know, I've always, I've always felt you had to, to take *action*, not sit, not to be, to be trapped, um, stuck, paralyzed by— Even if it's hard, or really terrifying, or even if it does damage, you have to keep moving, um, forward, instead of— I can't just, you know, sit around *feeling* shit, or feeling *like* shit, I . . . cry way too easily, I fall apart, I'm no good unless I, I *strike out* at— Which is easy because I'm so fucking *furious* at my— So I fucked up spectacularly, totally, I've ruined my life, and his life, I've hurt him so badly but but still, even I, even I am not so utterly lost inside myself that I— I wouldn't, um, *ever*, like, *sleep* with someone who . . . someone who's *Roy Cohn's* . . . *(He stops himself)*

BELIZE: Buttboy.

LOUIS *(In complete despair, quietly)*: Oh no.

BELIZE: You know what your problem is, Louis? Your problem is that you are so full of piping hot crap that the mention of your name draws flies. You don't even know Thing One about this guy, do you?

(Louis shakes his head no.)

BELIZE: Uh-huh. Well ain't that pathetic.

Just so's the record's straight: I love Prior but I was never in love with him. I have a man, uptown, and I have since *long* before I first laid my eyes on the sorry-ass sight of you.

LOUIS: I . . . I didn't know that you—

BELIZE: No 'cause you never bothered to ask.

Up in the air, just like that angel, too far off the earth to pick out the details. Louis and his Big Ideas. Big Ideas are all you love. "America" is what Louis loves.

(Louis is looking at the angel, not at Belize.)

LOUIS: So what? Maybe I do. You don't know what I love.
You don't.

BELIZE: Well I hate America, Louis. I hate this country. It's just big ideas, and stories, and people dying, and people like you.

The white cracker who wrote the National Anthem knew what he was doing. He set the word "free" to a note so high nobody can reach it. That was deliberate. Nothing on earth sounds less like freedom to me.

You come with me to room 1013 over at the hospital, I'll show you America. Terminal, crazy and mean.

(A rumble of thunder. Then the rain comes. Belize has a collapsible umbrella, and he raises it. Louis stands in the rain.)

BELIZE: I *live* in America, Louis, that's hard enough, I don't have to love it. You do that. Everybody's got to love something.

(Belize leaves.)

LOUIS *(Quiet, resolved)*: Everybody does.

Scene 6

Same day. Hannah sits alone at the Visitors' Center reception desk.
It's dark outside, and raining steadily. Distant thunder.
  Joe enters.
  They look at each other for a long moment.

JOE: You shouldn't have come.

HANNAH: You already made that clear as day.

JOE: I'm sorry. I . . . I . . . don't understand why you're here.

HANNAH: For more than two weeks. You can't even return a simple phone call.

JOE: I just don't . . . have anything to say. I have nothing to say.

HANNAH: You could tell me so I could tell her where you are. You've been living on some rainy rooftop for all we knew. It's cruel.

JOE: Not intended to be.

HANNAH: You're sure about that.

JOE: I'm taking her home.

HANNAH: You think that's best for her, you think that she should—

JOE: I know what I'm doing.

HANNAH: I don't think you have a clue. You can afford not to. You're a man, you botch up, it's not a big deal, but she's been—

JOE: Just being a man doesn't mean . . . anything.
  It's still a big deal, Ma. Botching up.
  (Tough, cold, angry, holding it in) And nothing works. Not all my . . . oh, you know, my *effortful* clinging to the good, to what's right, not pursuing . . . freedom, or happiness. Nothing, nothing works anymore, nothing I try

fixes anything at all, nothing, I've got nothing, now, my whole life, all I've done is make . . . botches. Just . . .

(He looks down, shakes his head; he can't continue. Then:)
I'm really . . . um . . . *(This is not the word he wants to say)* bewildered . . .

(Little pause. Hannah looks at him; he wants consolation, but something stops her.)

HANNAH *(Quietly but firmly)*: Being a woman's harder. Look at her.

(Little pause.)

JOE: You and me. It's like we're back in Salt Lake again. You sort of bring the desert with you.
Is she . . . ?

HANNAH: She's not here.

JOE: But . . . I went to the apartment. She isn't . . .

HANNAH: Then she's escaped.
I think maybe motion's better for her right now, being out and away from—

JOE: It's raining. She can't be out on her own.

HANNAH: Can I help look for—

JOE: There's nothing you can do. You should go, Ma, you should go back home. It's a terrible time. You never wanted to visit before. You shouldn't—

HANNAH: You never asked me.

JOE: You didn't have to—

HANNAH: I didn't and I shouldn't and I don't know *why* I did, but I'm here, so let me help.

JOE: *She's my responsibility. Ma.* Fly home. Please.

HANNAH: I . . . can't.

JOE: Why?

HANNAH: I . . .

Aunt Libby thought she'd smelled radon gas in the basement.

JOE: What?

HANNAH: Of the house.

JOE: You can't smell radon gas, it has no smell, and since when do you listen to, to Libby? I can't— *(Continue below:)*

HANNAH: I acted on impulse, and I . . . *(She decides against telling him that she's sold the house)*

JOE *(Continuous from above)*: I can't, um, could we talk about this another—

HANNAH: That thing you told me, that night. On the telephone, from Central Park. When you were drinking.

JOE: No, we can't do that. Not now. I don't want to— *(Continue below:)*

HANNAH: You said you thought you—

JOE *(Continuous from above)*: I don't want to talk about it. Forget it.

HANNAH: But I think maybe now we ought to, we ought to—

JOE *(Suddenly scarily enraged)*: NO!! And do what?! PRAY TOGETHER?! *NO.* I couldn't . . . *stomach* the prospect!

(Hannah turns away. He stares, baffled; it takes several moments for him to realize she might be crying.)

JOE: Are you . . . ?

I'm sorry. Don't cry.

HANNAH *(Not turning to face him)*: Don't be stupid.

And if I ever do. I promise you you'll not be privileged to witness it.

JOE: I should . . .

(Still facing away, she nods yes.)

JOE: Is there radon gas in the—
HANNAH: Just go.

(Little pause.)

JOE: I'll pay to change your ticket.

(Joe exits. Hannah sits. She's alone for several moments. There's a peal of thunder.
    Prior enters, wet, in his prophet garb, dark glasses on, despite the dark day outside. He's breathless, manic.)

PRIOR: That man who was just here.
HANNAH *(Not looking at him)*: We're closed. Go away.
PRIOR: He's your son.

(Hannah looks at Prior. Little pause. Prior turns to leave.)

HANNAH: Do you know him. That man?
    How . . . How do you know him, that he's my—
PRIOR: My ex-boyfriend, he knows him. I, I shadowed him, all the way up from— I wanted to, to . . . warn him about *later*, when his hair goes and there's hips and jowls and all that . . . human stuff, that poor slob there's just gonna wind up miserable, fat, frightened and *alone* because Louis, he can't handle bodies.

(Little pause.)

HANNAH: Are you a . . . a homosexual?
PRIOR: Oh is it *that* obvious? Yes. I am. What's it to you?

HANNAH: Would you say you are a typical . . . homosexual?

PRIOR: Me? Oh I'm *stereotypical*. What, you mean like am I a hairdresser or . . .

HANNAH: *Are* you a hairdresser?

PRIOR: Well it would be *your* lucky day if I was because frankly . . .

(Little pause.)

PRIOR: I'm sick. I'm sick. It's expensive.
(He starts to cry)
Oh shit now I won't be able to stop, now it's started. I feel really terrible, do I have a fever?

(Hannah doesn't touch his forehead. He offers it again, impatiently.)

PRIOR: *Do I have a fever?*

(She hesitates, then puts her hand on his forehead.)

HANNAH: Yes.

PRIOR: How high?

HANNAH: There might be a thermometer in the—

PRIOR: Very high, very high. Could you get me to a cab, I think I want . . .
(He sits heavily on the floor)
Don't be alarmed, it's worse than it looks, I mean—

HANNAH: You should . . . Try to stand up, or . . . Let me see if anyone can—

PRIOR *(Listening to his lungs)*: Sssshhh.
Echo-breath, it's . . . *(He shakes his head "no good")* I . . . overdid it. I'm in trouble again.

Take me to Saint Vincent's Hospital, I mean, help me to a cab to the . . .

(Little pause, then Hannah exits and reenters with her coat on.)

HANNAH: Can you stand up?
PRIOR: You don't . . . Call me a—
HANNAH: I'm useless here.

(She helps him stand.)

PRIOR: Please, if you're trying to convert me this isn't a good time.

(Distant thunder. Prior looks up, startled.)

HANNAH: Lord, look at it out there. It's pitch-black. We better move.

(They exit. Thunder.)

Scene 7

Same day, late afternoon. Rain is coming down in sheets, an icy wind has picked up. Harper is standing at the railing of the Promenade in Brooklyn Heights, watching the river and the Manhattan skyline. She is wearing the dress she wore in Act Three, Scene 3, inadequate for the weather, and she's barefoot.
Joe enters with an umbrella. Harper turns to face him.

HARPER: The end of the world is at hand. Hello, paleface. *(She turns back to the skyline)*

Nothing like storm clouds over Manhattan to get you in the mood for Judgment Day.

(Thunder.)

JOE: It's freezing, it's raining, where are your shoes?
HARPER: I threw them in the river.

The Judgment Day. Everyone will think they're crazy now, not just me, everyone will see things. Sick men will see angels, women who have houses will sell their houses, dime store dummies will rear up on their wood-putty legs and roam the land, looking for brides.
JOE: Let's go home.
HARPER: Where's that?

(Pointing toward Manhattan) Want to buy an island? It's going out of business. You can have it for the usual cheap trinkets. Fire sale. The prices are insane.
JOE: Harper.
HARPER: Joe. Did you miss me?
JOE: I . . . I've come back.
HARPER: Oh I know.

Here's why I wanted to stay in Brooklyn. The Promenade view.

Water won't ever accomplish the end. No matter how much you cry. Flood's not the answer, people just float.

Let's go home.

Fire's the answer. The Great and Terrible Day. At last.

Scene 8

That night. Rain and thunder outside. Prior, Hannah and Emily (Prior's nurse-practitioner) in an examination room in Saint Vincent's emergency room. Emily is listening to Prior's breathing, while Hannah sits in a nearby chair.

EMILY: You've lost eight pounds. Eight pounds! I know people who would kill to be in the shape you were in, you were *recovering*, and you threw it away.

PRIOR: This isn't about WEIGHT, it's about LUNGS, UM . . . PNEUMONIA.

EMILY: We don't know yet.

PRIOR: THE FUCK WE DON'T ASSHOLE YOU MAY NOT BUT I *CAN'T BREATHE.*

HANNAH: You'd breathe better if you didn't holler like that.

PRIOR *(Looks at Hannah, then)*: This is my ex-lover's lover's Mormon mother.

(Little pause. Emily nods, then:)

EMILY: Keep breathing. Stop moving. STAY PUT.

(Prior startles at her last two words, and stares hard at Emily as she exits.)

HANNAH *(Standing to go)*: I should go.

PRIOR: I'm not insane.

HANNAH: I didn't say you—

PRIOR: I saw an angel.

(She doesn't respond.)

PRIOR: That's insane.

HANNAH: Well, it's—

PRIOR: Insane. But I'm not insane. Do I *seem* insane?

HANNAH: You . . . I'm not sure I—

PRIOR: Oh for pityfuckingsake just answer the fucking—

HANNAH: No. *Driven*, and, and rude, but—

PRIOR: But then why did I do this to myself? Because I have been driven insane by . . . your son and by that lying . . . Because I'm consumed by this ice-cold, razorblade terror that shouts and shouts, "Don't stay still get out of bed keep moving! Run!" And I've run myself into the ground. Right where She said I'd eventually be.

   What's happened to me?

   She seemed so real.

HANNAH: Who?

   Oh, the . . . *(Angel gesture)*

(Prior nods yes.
   Hannah hesitates, then:)

HANNAH: Could be you had a vision.

PRIOR: A vision. Thank you, Maria Ouspenskaya.

HANNAH: People have visions.

PRIOR: No they— Not sane people.

HANNAH *(A beat before deciding to say this)*: One hundred and seventy years ago, which is recent, an angel of God appeared to Joseph Smith. In Upstate New York, not far from here.

PRIOR: But that's ridiculous, that's—

HANNAH: It's not polite to call other people's beliefs ridiculous.

PRIOR: I didn't mean to—

HANNAH: I *believe* this. He had great need of understanding. Our Prophet. His desire made prayer. His prayer made an angel. The angel was real. I believe that.

PRIOR: I don't. And I'm sorry but it's repellent to me. So much of what you believe.

HANNAH: What do I believe?

PRIOR: I'm a homosexual. With AIDS. I can just imagine what you—

HANNAH: No you can't. Imagine. The things in my head. You don't make assumptions about me, mister; I won't make them about you.

PRIOR *(A beat; he looks at her, then)*: Fair enough.

HANNAH: My son is . . . well, like you.

PRIOR: Homosexual.

HANNAH *(A nod, then)*: I flew into a rage when he told me, mad as August hornets. At first I assumed it was about his . . . *(She shrugs)*

PRIOR: Homosexuality.

HANNAH: But that wasn't it. Homosexuality. I don't find it an appetizing notion, two men, together, but men in *any* configuration . . . That wasn't it. Stupidity gets me cross, but that wasn't it either. I flew into a rage, filled with rage, then the rage . . . lifted me up; I felt . . . Truly I felt lifted up, into the air, and . . .

(She laughs to herself)

And I flew.

PRIOR: I wish you would be more true to your demographic profile.

(Little pause. Hannah smiles. They both laugh, a little. Prior's laugh brings on breathing trouble. Trying to find a comfortable position, he begins to panic.)

HANNAH: Just lie still. You'll be all right.

PRIOR: No. I won't be. My lungs are getting tighter. The fever mounts and you get delirious. And then days of delirium and awful pain and drugs; you start slipping and then.

I really . . . fucked up.

(Losing it, crying) I'm scared. I can't do it again.

HANNAH: You shouldn't talk that way. You ought to make a better show of yourself.

PRIOR: Look at this . . . horror.

(He lifts his shirt; his torso is spotted with several lesions)
See? See that? That's not human. That's why I run.

(Hannah's shocked but doesn't show it; it's hard to look at, but she manages.)

HANNAH: It's a cancer. Nothing more. Nothing more human than that.

(She puts a hand on his shoulder. He calms down. They're silent for a moment.)

PRIOR: Do Mormons read the you know the Bible? Or just the—

HANNAH *(Tight, trying not to take offense)*: The Book of Mormon is a part of the—

PRIOR: Don't get technical, you know what I mean, the other parts, the Old Testament part.

HANNAH: I've read the—

PRIOR: The prophets in the Bible, do they . . . ever refuse their visions?

HANNAH *(Considering, then)*: One did. There might be others, I—

PRIOR: And what does God do to them? When they do that?
HANNAH: He . . . feeds them to whales.

(Prior laughs, Hannah joins him, they're both a little hysterical. The laughter subsides.)

PRIOR: Stay with me.
HANNAH: Oh no, I—
PRIOR: Just till I sleep? You comfort me.
HANNAH: Oh, I—
PRIOR: You do, you . . . *(A little Katharine Hepburn)* stiffen my spine.

(Little pause.)

HANNAH: I'm not needed elsewhere, I suppose I . . .
  (She thinks for a moment, then sits in a chair)
  When I got up this morning this is not how I envisioned the day would end.
PRIOR: Me neither.

(He lies back, and she settles into her chair.)

HANNAH: An angel is a belief. With wings and arms that can carry you. If it lets you down, reject it.

(Prior looks at her.)

PRIOR: Huh.
HANNAH: There's scriptural precedent.
PRIOR: And then what?
HANNAH *(A little shrug, then)*: Seek something new.

Scene 9

*That night, the rain's still falling. The Pitt apartment in Brooklyn.
Joe and Harper's clothing is strewn about the floor.*

    *Joe enters from the bedroom in a pair of boxers. He picks up
his shirt, puts it on and starts to button it. He stops when Harper
enters, wrapped in a bedsheet, naked underneath. He hesitates a
beat, then resumes buttoning.*

HARPER: When we have sex. Why do you keep your eyes closed?
JOE: I don't.
HARPER: You always do. You can say why, I already know the
    answer.
JOE: Then why do I have to—
HARPER: You imagine things.
    Imagine men.
JOE: Yes.
HARPER: Imagining, just like me, except the only time I wasn't
    imagining was when I was with you. You, the one part of
    the real world I wasn't allergic to.
JOE: Please. Don't.
HARPER: But I only *thought* I wasn't dreaming.

    *(Joe picks up his pants. Harper watches him as he puts them
on, then:)*

HARPER: Oh. Oh. Back in Brooklyn, back with Joe.
JOE *(Still dressing, not looking at Harper)*: I'm going out. I have
    to get some stuff I left behind.
HARPER: Look at me.

    (He doesn't. He puts on his socks and shoes.)

HARPER: Look at me.

Look at me.

Here! Look here at—

JOE *(Looking at her)*: *What?*

HARPER: What do you see?

JOE: What do I . . . ?

HARPER: What do you see?

JOE: *Nothing, I—*

(Little pause)

I see nothing.

HARPER *(A nod, then)*: Finally. The truth.

JOE *(A beat, then)*: I'm going. Out. Just . . . Out.

(He exits.)

HARPER: It sets you free.

Good-bye.

Scene 10

Later that night. Louis is in his apartment, sitting on the floor; all around him are Xeroxed pages stapled together in thick packets. Louis is reading one of these.

There's a knock at the door.

JOE *(Outside the apartment)*: Louis.

Please let me in.

(Louis looks at the Xeroxed packets, fixes a grim little smile on his face, stands, unlocks the door, then immediately returns to his place on the floor.)

LOUIS: You're in.

(A little pause, then Joe turns the knob, opens the door and enters. He looks at Louis, who's ignoring him, continuing to read.)

JOE: You weren't at work. For three days now. You . . . I wish you'd get a phone.

    I'm staying in a hotel, near Fulton Street. It's kind of—

    You said you'd call me, or—

LOUIS *(Still reading)*: No I never.

JOE: Or OK I expected you to call me, I hoped you'd—

LOUIS *(Finally looking at Joe)*: "Have you no decency, sir?"

    Who said that?

JOE: I'm having a very hard time. With this. Please, can we—

LOUIS: "At long last? Have you no sense of decency?"

    (Fake pleasant teasing) Come on, who said it?

JOE: Who said . . . ?

LOUIS: Who said, "Have you no—"

JOE: I don't . . . I'm not interested in playing guessing games, Louis, please stop and let me—

LOUIS: You *really* don't know who said, "Have you no decency?"

JOE: I want to tell you something, I want to—

LOUIS: OK, second question: *Have* you no decency?

(Joe doesn't respond. Louis gathers the Xeroxed packets and stands up.)

LOUIS: Guess what I spent the rainy afternoon doing?

JOE: What?

LOUIS: Research at the courthouse. Look what I got:

    (Holding out the papers) The Decisions of Justice Theodore Wilson, Second Circuit Court of Appeals. 1981–1984. The Reagan Years.

(Little pause.)

JOE: You, um, you read my decisions.

LOUIS: *Your* decisions. Yes.

(The fake pleasantness fading) The librarian's gay, he has all the good dish, he told me that Justice Wilson didn't write these opinions any more than Nixon wrote *Six Crises*—

JOE: Or Kennedy wrote *Profiles in Courage.*

LOUIS: Or Reagan wrote *Where's the Rest of Me?* Or you and I wrote the Book of Love.

These gems were ghostwritten. By you: his obedient clerk.

JOE: OK, OK so we can talk about the decisions, if that's what you want, or, or Prior, if you want to talk about— If you saw him, I'm— Well I'm relieved you're here. I was scared you'd have moved back, I mean out. I'm . . . Oh God it's so good to see you again.

(Joe tries to touch Louis. Louis puts a hand on Joe's chest and firmly pushes him back.)

JOE: Hey!

LOUIS: Naturally I was eager to read them.

(Louis starts flipping through the files, looking for one in particular.)

JOE: Free country.

LOUIS *(Finding it, leafing through the pages)*: I love the one where you found against those women on Staten Island who were suing the New Jersey factory, the toothpaste makers whose orange-colored smoke was *blinding children*—

JOE: Not blind, just minor irritation.

(Louis holds the decision right up to Joe's face, open to the relevant page.)

LOUIS: Three of them had to be hospitalized. Joe.

(Joe looks away from the paper.)

LOUIS: It's sort of brilliant, in a satanic sort of way, how you conclude— *(Continue below:)*
JOE: I don't believe this.
LOUIS *(Continuous from above)*: —How you concluded that these women had no right to sue under the Air and Water Protection Act because—
JOE: My opinions are being criticized by the guy who changes the coffee filters in the secretaries' lounge!
LOUIS: Because the Air and Water Protection Act doesn't protect *people*, but actually only *air and water*. That's like— *(Continue below:)*
JOE: It's not your fault that you have no idea what you're talking about— *(Continue below:)*
LOUIS *(Continuous from above)*: That's like fucking *creative*, or something.
     (Under his breath while flipping through the cases) Have you no decency, have you no—
JOE *(Continuous from above)*: —but it's unbelievable to me how total ignorance is no impediment for you in forming half-baked uninformed snap judgments masquerading as adult opinions, you, you . . . *child*.

(Joe snatches at the papers. Louis dodges, at the same time locating the case he's been looking for.)

LOUIS: But my *absolute favorite* is this:
Stephens versus the United States.

JOE: Of course. I was waiting for that. It's a complicated case, you don't—

LOUIS: The army guy who got a dishonorable discharge— for being gay. Now as I understand it, this Stephens had told the army he was gay when he enlisted, but when he got ready to retire they booted him out. Cheat the queer of his pension.

JOE: Right. And he sued. And he won the case. He got the pension back. And then the—

LOUIS: The first judges gave him his pension back, *yes*, because: they ruled that gay men are members of a legitimate minority, entitled to the special protection of the Fourteenth Amendment of the U.S. Constitution. Equal Protection under the Law.

I can just imagine how that momentary lapse into you know *sanity* was received! So then all the judges on the Second Circuit were *hastily* assembled, and—

JOE: And they found for the guy again, they—

LOUIS: But but but!

On an equitable estoppel. I had to look that up, I'm Mr. Coffee, I can't be expected to know these things. They didn't change the *decision*, they just changed the *reason for* the decision. Right? They gave it to him on a technicality: the army knew Stephens was gay when he enlisted. That's all, that's why he won. Not because it's unconstitutional to discriminate against homosexuals. Because homosexuals, they write, are *not* entitled to equal protection under the law.

JOE: Not, not insofar as precedence determines the—which is how law works, as opposed to— The definition of a suspect class, which you probably've never—

LOUIS: Actually *they* didn't write this.

(He goes right up to Joe; speaking softly) You did. They gave this opinion to Wilson to write, which since they *know* he's a vegetable incapable of writing do-re-mi, was quite the vote of confidence in his industrious little sidekick. This is an important bit of legal fag-bashing, isn't it? They trusted you to do it. And you didn't disappoint.

JOE: It's law not justice, it's power, not the merits of its exercise, it's not an expression of the ideal, it's—

LOUIS: So who said, "Have you no decency?"

JOE: I didn't come here to— I'm leaving.

(Joe starts toward the door. Louis gets in his way.)

LOUIS: You moron, how can you not know that?

JOE: I'm leaving, you . . . son of a bitch, get out of my—

LOUIS: It's only the greatest punchline in American history.

JOE *(Very angry, threatening)*: Out of my way, Louis.

LOUIS: *"Have you no decency, at long last, sir, have you no decency at all?"*

JOE: I DON'T KNOW WHO SAID IT! Why are you doing this to me?! *I love you!* Please believe me, please, *I love you. Stop hurting me like—*

LOUIS: *Joseph Welch!* The Army/McCarthy hearings!

Ask Roy. He'll tell you. He knows. He was *there.*

(Little pause)

Roy Cohn. What I want to know is, did you fuck him?

JOE: Did I what?

LOUIS: How often has the latex-sheathed cock I put in my mouth been previously in the mouth of the most evil, twisted, vicious bastard ever to snort coke at Studio 54, because lips that kissed those lips will never kiss mine.

JOE: Don't worry about that, just get out of the—

(Joe tries to push Louis aside; Louis pushes back, forcefully.)

LOUIS: Did you fuck him, did he pay you to let him—
JOE: MOVE!

(Louis throws the Xeroxes in Joe's face. They fly everywhere. Joe pushes Louis, Louis grabs Joe.)

LOUIS: You *lied* to me, you *love* me, well fuck you, you cheap piece of—

(Joe shoves Louis aside. Louis stumbles as Joe starts for the door.)

LOUIS: He's got AIDS!

(Joe stops.)

LOUIS: Did you even *know* that?

(Joe starts again for the door, but Louis grabs him. They struggle.)

LOUIS: Stupid closeted bigots, you probably never figured out that each other was—
JOE: Shut up.

(Joe slugs Louis in the stomach, hard. Louis goes to his knees. Again Joe tries to leave, but Louis grabs his leg and won't let go. Louis pulls himself up, using Joe's leg and jacket, as Joe struggles to free himself.)

LOUIS: Fascist hypocrite lying filthy—

(Joe punches Louis in the face. Louis drops to the floor, clutching his eye. Joe stands over him.)

JOE: Now stop. Now stop. I . . .

LOUIS: Oh jeeesus, aw jeez, oh . . .

JOE: Please. Say you're OK, please. *Please.*

LOUIS: That . . . Hurt.

JOE: I never did that before, I never hit anyone before, I—

(Louis sits up. One eye has been cut. Blood's running down his face.)

JOE: Can you open it? Can you see?

LOUIS: I can see blood.

JOE: Let me get a towel, let me—

LOUIS: I could have you arrested you . . . Creep.

They'd think I put you in jail for beating me up.

JOE: I never hit anyone before, I—

LOUIS: But it'd really be for those decisions.

(Laughing) It was like a sex scene in an Ayn Rand novel, huh?

JOE: I hurt you. I'm sorry, Louis, I never hit anyone before, I . . .

(Joe tries to touch Louis. Louis shoves Joe's hand away.)

LOUIS: Yeah yeah get lost. Before I really lose my temper and hurt you back.

I just want to lie here and bleed for a while. Do me good.

(Joe stands still, not knowing what to do. He looks at his hand, which he's hurt in the fight; there's blood on it.

He looks at Louis, then starts to leave, then stops. He stares
at Louis, unable to move.
Then he leaves.)

Scene 11

Later that night. Roy in a very serious hospital bed, monitoring
machines and IV drips galore. Ethel appears.

ROY *(Very weak, singing to himself)*:
John Brown's body lies a-moulderin' in the grave,
John Brown's body lies a-moulderin' in the grave,
John Brown's body lies a-moulderin' in the grave,
His truth is marching on . . .

ETHEL: Look at that big smile. What you got to smile about,
Roy?

ROY: I'm going, Ethel. Finally, finally done with this world, at
long long last. All mine enemies will be standing on the
other shore, mouths gaping open like stupid fish, while
the Almighty parts the Sea of Death and lets his Royboy
cross over to Jordan. On dry land and still a lawyer.

ETHEL: Don't count your chickens, Roy.
It's over.

ROY: Over?

ETHEL: I wanted the news should come from me.
The panel ruled against you Roy.

ROY: No, no, they only started meeting two days ago.

ETHEL: They recommended disbarment.

ROY: The Executive still has to rule . . . on the recommendation,
it'll take another week to sort it out and before then—

ETHEL: The Executive was waiting, and they ruled, one two three. They accepted the panel's recommendation.

ROY *(A beat, then)*: I'm . . .

ETHEL: One of the main guys on the Executive leaned over to his friend and said, "Finally. I've hated that little faggot for thirty-six years."

ROY: I'm . . . They . . . ?

ETHEL: They won, Roy. You're not a lawyer anymore.

ROY: But am I dead?

ETHEL: No. They beat you. You lost.

(Pause)

I decided to come here so I could see could I forgive you. You who I have hated so terribly I have borne my hatred for you up into the heavens and made a needle-sharp little star in the sky out of it. It's the star of Ethel Rosenberg's Hatred, and it burns every year for one night only, June Nineteen. It burns acid green.

(Roy has turned his face away from her, looking in the opposite direction.)

ETHEL: I came to forgive but all I can do is take pleasure in your misery. Hoping I'd get to see you die more terrible than I did. And you are, 'cause you're dying in shit, Roy, defeated. And you could kill me, but you couldn't ever defeat me. You never won. And when you die all anyone will say is: Better he had never lived at all.

(Pause. Roy slowly turns his head back to stare at Ethel.)

ROY: Ma?

Muddy? Is it . . . ?

Ma?

ETHEL *(Uncertain, then)*: It's Ethel, Roy.

ROY: Muddy? I feel bad.

ETHEL *(Looking around)*: Who are you talking to, Roy, it's—

ROY: Good to see you, Ma, it's been years.

I feel bad. Sing to me.

ETHEL: I'm not your mother, Roy.

ROY: It's cold in here, I'm up so late, past my time.

Don't be mad, Ma, but I'm scared . . . ? A little.

Don't be mad. Sing me a song. Please.

ETHEL: I don't want to Roy, I'm not your—

ROY: Please, it's scary out here. *(He starts to cry)*

(He sinks back) Oh God. Oh God, I'm so sorry . . .

(Little pause.)

ETHEL *(Singing softly)*:

Shteyt a bocher

Un er tracht,

Tracht un tracht

A gantze nacht:

Vemen tzu nemen

Um nit farshemen

Vemen tsu nemen,

Um nit farshem.

Tum-ba-la, tum-ba-la, tum-balalaike,

Tum-ba-la, tum-ba-la, tum-balalaike,

Tum-balalaike, shpil balalaike—

(Roy is completely still, his eyes closed. He's not breathing. Ethel watches him; then, quietly:)

ETHEL: Roy . . . ? Are you . . . ?

(She crosses to the bed, looks at him. Goes back to her chair.)

ETHEL: That's it.

(Belize enters, goes to the bed.)

BELIZE: Wake up, it's time to—
Oh.
Oh, you're—

(Roy's eyes pop open and he sits bolt upright!)

ROY: No I'm *NOT*!
(Shaking with some terrible, jubilant, hateful joy) I fooled
you, Ethel! I knew who you were all along! I can't believe
you fell for that Ma stuff!! I just wanted to see if I could
finally, *finally* make Ethel Rosenberg sing! *I WIN!*
*(Something very bad happens in his head—he's thrown
a pulmonary clot, and it strikes his brain—and he falls back
on the bed)*
Oh fuck, oh fuck me I—
(In a faraway voice, to Belize) Next time around: I don't
want to be a man. I wanna be an octopus. Remember
that, OK? A fucking— *(Punching an imaginary button
with his finger)* Hold.

(Roy dies.)

ACT FIVE:

Heaven,
I'm in Heaven

January 1986

Scene 1

Very late, same night. Prior has been moved to a proper hospital room. He's standing on his bed, a pillow covering his crotch. There's an eerie light on him. Hannah is sleeping in a chair, a flimsy hospital blanket covering her lap and legs. She stirs, moans a little, wakes up suddenly, sees Prior.

PRIOR: She's approaching.
HANNAH: What are you . . . ?
    She is?
PRIOR: Modesty forbids me explaining exactly *how* I know, but . . . I have an infallible barometer of Her proximity. And it's rising.

HANNAH: Oh, nonsense, that's—

PRIOR: She's on Her way.

(The lights drain to black.)

HANNAH: Turn the lights back on, turn the lights—

(There is the sound of a silvery trumpet in the dark, and a tattoo of faraway drums. Silence. Thunder. Then all over the walls, Hebrew letters appear, writhing in flames. The scene is lit by their light. The Angel is there, suddenly. She is dressed in black and looks terrifying. Hannah screams and buries her face in her hands.)

ANGEL: I I I I Have Returned, Prophet,
   (Thunder!)
   And not according to Plan.

PRIOR: Take it back.
   (Big thunderclap)
   The Book, whatever you left in me, I won't be its repository, I reject it.
   (Thunder. To Hannah:)
   Help me out here. HELP ME!

HANNAH *(Closing her eyes tight, trying to shut it all out)*: I don't, I don't— *(Pulling the blanket over her head)* This is a dream it's a dream it's a—

PRIOR: I don't think that's really the point right at this particular—

HANNAH *(Under the blanket)*: I don't know what to—

PRIOR: Well it was *your* idea, reject the vision you said and—
   (Continue below:)

HANNAH: Yes but I thought it was more a . . . metaphorical . . . I—

PRIOR *(Continuous from above)*: You said scriptural precedent, you said—

(Prior tries to yank the blanket away from Hannah, who hangs on to it.)

PRIOR: WHAT AM I SUPPOSED TO—

HANNAH: You, you wrestle her.

PRIOR: SAY *WHAT*?

HANNAH: It's an angel, you just . . . grab hold and say . . . oh what was it, wait, wait, umm . . . OH! Grab her, say, "I will not let thee go except thou bless me!"

PRIOR: And then what?

HANNAH: Then wrestle with her till she gives in.

PRIOR *(A beat, then)*: YOU wrestle Her, I don't know how to wrestle, I—

(Prior faces the Angel, who has been waiting for him, blazing with menace. She opens her arms, challenging, terrifying. Prior draws as deep a breath as he can; then, to his and her and Hannah's surprise, he charges at the Angel. He throws his arms around her waist. She emits a terrible, impossibly loud, shuddering eagle-screech.)

PRIOR: I . . . will not let thee go except thou bless me.

(She tries to pry him off, but he hangs on. Prior and the Angel begin to wrestle. It is a life-and-death struggle, fierce, violent and deadly serious. The Angel at first is far stronger and has a clear upper hand. But she cannot pry Prior loose. As they struggle:)

PRIOR: Take back . . . your Book. Anti-Migration, that's . . . so . . . *feeble*, I can't believe . . . you couldn't do better than that!

(Prior's tenacity begins to tire and panic her. She screeches again, then unable to shake him off, she opens her wings wide and begins to beat them, battering Prior. He loses his grip for an instant; she rises immediately into the air. Prior leaps up, grabs her right leg and pulls down with all his might and weight. She beats her wings more furiously, rising higher, lifting him up off the ground, but he won't let go.)

PRIOR: Free me! Unfetter me! Bless me or whatever . . . but *I will be let go.*

(The Angel is straining Heavenward but can't ascend higher; Prior's weight causes her to lose altitude.)

ANGEL *(Her voice a whole chorus of voices)*: I I I I Am the
CONTINENTAL PRINCIPALITY OF
AMERICA, I I I I
AM THE BIRD OF PREY I Will NOT BE
COMPELLED, I—

(They descend. Prior's feet touch earth first, and he redoubles his grasp, first on her leg and then her torso, wrapping himself tightly around her. Helpless, she stretches her wings to their utmost, screams the eagle-screech again, and stops fighting.

Instantly there is a great blast of music. The fiery letters fade and the room is sunk in blue murk. A second blast of music, even louder, and, from above, a column of incredibly bright white light stabs through the blue. Within the column of light, a ladder of even brighter, purer light appears, reaching up into infinity. At the conjunctions of each rung there are flaming Alephs.)

ANGEL: Entrance has been gained. Return the Text to Heaven.
PRIOR *(Terrified)*: Can I come back? I don't want to go unless—

ANGEL *(Very angry)*: You have prevailed, Prophet. You . . . *Choose!*

Now release me.

I have torn a muscle in my thigh.

PRIOR: Big deal, my leg's been hurting for months.

(He releases the Angel. He hesitates. He looks at Hannah, asking her: "Should I go?" Frightened as she is, she manages to hold her hand out, bidding him to stay.

Prior, suddenly very sad, shakes his head no, and turns to the ladder. After one last look at the Angel, he puts his hands on the rungs, then one foot, then the other, and begins climbing. The column of bright light intensifies as he ascends, till Prior and the ladder are entirely subsumed within its blinding radiance and can no longer be seen.

Then abruptly the column of light disappears, and the room is drowned in semi-darkness. The ladder and Prior are gone. The Angel turns to Hannah.)

HANNAH: What? What? You've got no business with me, I didn't call you, you're *his* fever dream not mine, and he's gone now and you should go, too, I'm waking up right . . . NOW!

(Nothing happens. The Angel spreads her wings. The room becomes red hot. The Angel extends her hands toward Hannah. Hannah walks toward her, torn between immense unfamiliar desire and fear. Hannah kneels. The Angel kisses her on the forehead and then the lips—a long, hot kiss.)

ANGEL: The Body is the Garden of the Soul.

(Hannah has an enormous orgasm, as the Angel flies away to the accompanying glissando of a baroque piccolo trumpet.)

Scene 2

Prior Walter is in Heaven. He wears new prophet robes, red, dark brown and white stripes, reminiscent of Charlton Heston's Moses-parting-the-Red-Sea drag in The Ten Commandments. *Beneath the robe, Prior's wearing his flimsy white hospital gown. He's carrying the Book of the Anti-Migratory Epistle.*

Heaven looks like San Francisco after the Great Quake: deserted streets, beautiful buildings in ruins, toppled telegraph poles, downed electrical cables, rubble strewn everywhere.

On a nearby street corner, Harper sits on a wooden crate, holding and petting a cat.

HARPER: Oh! It's you! My imaginary friend.

PRIOR: What are you doing here? Are you dead?

HARPER: No, I just had sex, I'm not dead! Why? Where are we?

PRIOR: Heaven.

HARPER: Heaven? I'm in Heaven?

PRIOR: That cat! That's Little Sheba!

HARPER: She was wandering around. Everyone here wanders. Or they sit on crates, playing card games. Heaven. Holy moly.

PRIOR: How did Sheba die?

HARPER: Rat poison, hit by a truck, fight with an alley cat, cancer, another truck, old age, fell in the East River, heartworms and one last truck.

PRIOR: Then it's true? Cats really have nine lives?

HARPER: That was a joke. I don't know how she died, I don't talk to cats I'm not that crazy. Just upset. Or . . .

We had sex, and then he . . . had to go. I drank an enormous glass of water and two Valiums. Or six. Maybe I overdosed, like Marilyn Monroe.

Did you die?

PRIOR: No, I'm here on business.

I can return to the world. If I want to.

HARPER: Do you?

PRIOR: I don't know.

HARPER: I know. Heaven is depressing, full of dead people and all, but life.

PRIOR: To face loss. With grace. Is key, I think, but it's impossible. All you ever do is lose and lose.

HARPER: But not letting go deforms you so.

PRIOR: The world's too hard. Stay here. With me.

HARPER: I can't. I feel like shit but I've never felt more alive. I've finally found the secret of all that Mormon energy. Devastation. That's what makes people migrate, build things. Devastated people do it, people who have lost love. Because I don't think God loves His people any better than Joe loved me. The string was cut, and off they went. Ravaged, heartbroken, and free.

(Little pause)

I have to go home now. I hope you come back. *Look* at this place. Can you imagine spending eternity here?

PRIOR: It's supposed to look like San Francisco.

HARPER *(Looking around)*: Ugh.

PRIOR: Oh but the real San Francisco, on earth, is unspeakably beautiful.

HARPER: Unspeakable beauty.

That's something I would like to see.

(Harper and Sheba vanish.)

PRIOR: Oh! She . . . She took the cat. Come back, you took the—

(Little pause)

Good-bye, Little Sheba. Good-bye.

(The Angel is standing there.)

ANGEL: Greetings, Prophet. We have been waiting for you.

Scene 3

Two A.M. Same night as Scene 1. Roy's hospital room. Roy's body is on the bed. Ethel is sitting in a chair. Belize enters, then calls off in a whisper:

BELIZE: Hurry.

> *(Louis enters wearing an overcoat and dark sunglasses, carrying an empty knapsack.)*

LOUIS: Oh my God, oh my God it's—oh this is too weird for words, it's Roy Cohn! It's . . . so *creepy* here, I hate hospitals, I—
BELIZE: *Stop whining.* We have to move fast, I'm supposed to call the duty nurse if his condition changes and . . . *(He looks at Roy)* It's changed.
> Take off those glasses you look ridiculous.

> *(Louis takes off the glasses. He has a black eye, with a nasty-looking cut above it.)*

BELIZE: What happened to *you?*

> *(Belize touches the swelling near Louis's eye.)*

LOUIS: OW OW! *(He waves Belize's hand away)* Expiation. For my sins. What am I doing here?

(Belize takes the knapsack from Louis.)

BELIZE: Expiation for your sins. I can't take the stuff out myself, I have to tell them he's dead and fill out all the forms, and I don't want them confiscating the medicine. I needed a packmule, so I called you.

LOUIS: Why me? You hate me.

BELIZE: I needed a Jew. You were the first to come to mind.

LOUIS: What do you mean you needed—

(Belize has opened Roy's refrigerator and begins putting all the bottles of AZT into the knapsack.)

BELIZE: We're going to thank him. For the pills.

LOUIS: *Thank him?*

BELIZE: What do you call the Jewish prayer for the dead?

LOUIS: The Kaddish?

BELIZE: That's the one. Hit it.

LOUIS: Whoah, hold on.

BELIZE: Do it, do it, they'll be in here to check and he—

(Belize has filled the knapsack and closed the empty refrigerator.)

LOUIS: I'm not— Fuck no! For *him*?! No fucking way! The drugs OK, sure, fine, but no fucking way am I praying for *him*. My New Deal Pinko Parents in Schenectady would never forgive me, they're already so disappointed, "He's a fag, he's an office temp, and *now look*, he's saying Kaddish for Roy Cohn." I can't believe you'd actually pray for—

BELIZE: Louis, I'd even pray for you.

He was a terrible person. He died a hard death. So maybe . . . A queen can forgive her vanquished foe. It isn't easy, it doesn't count if it's easy, it's the hardest thing. Forgiveness. Which is maybe where love and justice finally meet. Peace, at least. Isn't that what the Kaddish asks for?

LOUIS: Oh it's Hebrew or Aramaic or something, who knows what it's asking.

(Little pause. Louis and Belize look at each other, and then Louis looks at Roy, staring at him unflinchingly for the first time.)

LOUIS: I'm thirty-two years old and I've never seen a dead body before.
It's . . .

(Louis touches Roy's forehead.)

LOUIS: It's so heavy, and small.
(Little pause)
I know probably less of the Kaddish than you do, Belize, I'm an intensely secular Jew, I didn't even Bar Mitzvah.

BELIZE: Do the best you can.

(Louis hesitates, then puts a Kleenex on his head.)

LOUIS: Yisgadal ve'yiskadash sh'mey rabo, sh'mey de kidshoh, uh . . . Boray pre hagoffen. No, that's the Kiddush, not the . . . Um, shema Yisroel adonai . . . This is silly, Belize, I can't—

ETHEL *(Standing, softly)*: B'olmo deevro chiroosey ve'yamlich malchusey . . .

LOUIS: B'olmo deevro chiroosey ve'yamlich malchusey . . .

ETHEL: Bechayeychon uv'yomechechon uvchayey d'chol beys Yisroel . . .

LOUIS: Bechayeychon uv'yomechechon uvchayey d'chol beys
    Yisroel . . .

ETHEL: Ba'agolo uvizman koriv . . .

LOUIS: Ve'imroo omain.

ETHEL: Yehey sh'mey rabo m'vorach . . .

LOUIS AND ETHEL: L'olam ulolmey olmayoh. Yisborach
    ve'yishtabach ve'yispoar ve'yisroman ve'yisnasey ve'yis'-
    hadar ve'yisalleh ve'yishallol sh'mey dekudsho . . .

ETHEL: Berich hoo le'eylo min kol birchoso veshiroso . . .

ETHEL AND LOUIS: Tushbchoso venechemoso, daameeron
    b'olmo ve'imroo omain. Y'he sh'lomo rabbo min sh'mayo
    v'chayim olenu v'al kol Yisroel, v'imru omain.

ETHEL: Oseh sholom bimromov, hu ya-aseh sholom olenu v'al
    col Yisroel . . .

LOUIS: Oseh sholom bimromov, hu ya-aseh sholom olenu v'al
    col Yisroel . . .

ETHEL: V'imru omain.

LOUIS: V'imru omain.

ETHEL: You sonofabitch.

LOUIS: You sonofabitch.

(Ethel vanishes.
    Belize hands Louis the knapsack.)

BELIZE: Thank you, Louis. You did fine.

LOUIS: Fine? What are you talking about, fine? That was . . .
    fucking miraculous.

Scene 4

Two A.M. Joe enters the empty Brooklyn apartment.

JOE: I'm back. Harper?
>*(He switches on a light)*
>Harper?

>*(Roy enters from the bedroom, dressed in a fabulous floor-length black velvet robe de chambre. Joe starts with terror, turns away, then looks again. Roy's still there. Joe's terrified. Roy does not move.)*

JOE: What are you doing here?
ROY: Dead Joe doesn't matter.
JOE: No, no, you're not here, you . . .
>*(Joe closes his eyes, willing Roy away. He opens his eyes. Roy's still there)*
>You *lied* to me! You said cancer, you said—
ROY: You could have read it in the papers. AIDS. I didn't want you to get the wrong impression.
>You feel bad that you beat somebody.
JOE: I want you to—
ROY: He deserved it.
JOE: No he didn't, he—
ROY: Everybody does. Everybody could use a good beating.
JOE: No, no, that's— I want you to go Roy, you're really frightening me. *Get out.* You don't belong here—
>He didn't *deserve* what I did to him! I *hurt* him, Roy! I made him *bleed*! He . . . He won't ever see me again.

(Realizing that this is true) Oh no, oh no . . . What did I do that for? What did I do? What did I— *(Joe starts to cry. He stops himself, violently shaking his head)*
Tell me what to do now.

(Roy doesn't respond.)

JOE: I thought I was doing what I was supposed to do, I thought I'd find my way, the way you did, to the, to the heart of the things, to the heart of the world, I imagined myself . . . safe there, in the hollow of . . . but . . .
(Little pause)
I'm . . . above nothing. I'm . . . *of* the world. Whatever . . . that means, whatever God thinks of the world, I think He must think the same of me.
Tell me what I do now.

(Roy shrugs.)

JOE: I'm a liar. I lied. I never told you how much you frighten me, Roy.

(He walks toward Roy.)

JOE: I'm not blind, not . . . blind as I tried to be. I've always seen, *known* what you are. And, and I'm not like that. Not like you. But I've lied and lied and lied . . .

(Joe is facing Roy. He puts his head against Roy's chest, lost. Roy's surprised, pleased, moved. He puts his arms around Joe, a tender, careful embrace. Joe raises his head. They look at one another.)

ROY *(Gently)*: Show me a little of what you've learned, baby Joe. Out in the world.

(They kiss, intimate, uncertain, as affectionate as it is sexual.)

ROY: Damn.

> I gotta shuffle off this mortal coil.
>
> *(Looking up at the ceiling, warning the Powers Above:)* I hope they have something for me to do in the Great Hereafter, I get bored easy.
>
> *(To Joe)* You'll find, my friend, that what you love will take you places you never dreamed you'd go.

> *(Roy vanishes. Joe doesn't move, eyes closed.*
>
> *He opens them when Harper enters. They stare at one another.)*

HARPER: Hope you didn't worry.

JOE: Harper?

> Where . . . Were you—

HARPER: A trip to the moon on gossamer wings.

JOE: What?

HARPER: You ought to get your hearing checked, you say that a lot.

> I was out. With a friend. In Paradise.

Scene 5

Heaven: in the Council Room of the Hall of the Continental Principalities. As the scene is being set, a Voice proclaims:

A VOICE: In the Hall of the Continental Principalities; Heaven, a City Much Like San Francisco. Six of Seven Myriad Infinite Aggregate Angelic Entities in Attendance, May

Their Glorious Names Be Praised Forever and Ever, Hallelujah. Permanent Emergency Council is now in Session.

(Power for the great chamber is supplied by an unseen immense generator, the rhythmic pulsing as well as the occasional surges and wavers of which are visible in the unsteady lights, and audible continuously underneath the scene until its cessation [indicated in the text].

At the center of the room is a very large round table covered with a heavy tapestry on which is woven a seventeenth-century map of the world. The tabletop is covered with ancient and broken astronomical, astrological, mathematical and nautical objects of measurement and calculation, cracked clay tablets, dulled styli, dried inkpots, split quill pens, disintegrating piles of parchment, and old derelict typewriters. On the table and all around the room are heaps and heaps and heaps of books, bundles of yellowing newspapers and dusty teetery stacks of neglected and abandoned files.

On one side of the table, a single bulky radio, a 1940s model in very poor repair, is switched on, its dial and tubes glowing. The six present Continental Principalities are gathered about it, sitting and standing. The Angel of Asiatica is seated nearest to the radio; the Angel of Antarctica is farthest away.

The Principalities are dressed uniformly in elegant, flowing, severely black robes that look like what justices, judges, magistrates wear in court.

All six sound very much alike, as if speaking with a single voice. Their speech is always careful, a little slow, and soft, like mild old people; in everything they say there's a distinct tone of quiet, enduring desolation and perplexity. This tone doesn't vary; even when they argue they sound tentative, careful, broken.

They're almost completely still, but as they listen they turn slightly, slowly, looking to one another for comfort. Asiatica and Africanii intermittenly hold hands.

The Principalities are aghast, frightened and grief-stricken at the news they're hearing on the radio—which they're not supposed to be using. They listen intently to the dim, crackly signal.)

RADIO *(In a British accent)*: . . . one week following the explosion at the number four reactor, the fires are still burning and an estimated . . . *(Static)* . . . releasing into the atmosphere fifty million curies of radioactive iodine, six million curies of caesium and strontium rising in a plume over eight kilometers high, carried by the winds over an area stretching from the Urals to thousands of kilometers beyond Soviet borders, it . . . *(Static)*

ANTARCTICA: When?

OCEANIA: April 26th. Three months from today.

ASIATICA: Where is this place? This reactor?

EUROPA: Chernobyl. In Belarus.

(The static intensifies.)

ASIATICA: We are losing the signal.

(The Angels make mystic gestures. The signal returns.)

RADIO: . . . falling like toxic snow into the Dnieper River, which provides drinking water for thirty-five million— *(Static, then)* . . . is a direct consequence of the lack of safety culture caused by Cold War isolation— *(Static, then)* . . . Radioactive debris contaminating over three hundred thousand hectares of topsoil for a minimum of thirty years, and . . . *(Static)* . . . now hearing of thousands of workers who have absorbed fifty times the lethal dose of . . . *(Static)* . . . BBC Radio, reporting live from Chernobyl, on the eighth day of the . . .

(The radio signal is engulfed in white noise and fades out.)

EUROPA: Hundreds, thousands will die.

OCEANIA: Horribly. Hundreds of thousands.

AFRICANII: Millions.

ANTARCTICA: Let them. Uncountable multitudes. Horrible. It is by their own hands. I I I will rejoice to see it.

AUSTRALIA: That is forbidden us.
    Silence in Heaven.

ASIATICA: This radio is a terrible radio.

AUSTRALIA: The reception is too weak.

AFRICANII: A vacuum tube has died.

ASIATICA: Can it be fixed?

AUSTRALIA: It Is Beyond Us.

ASIATICA: However, I I I I I I I would like to know. What is a vacuum tube?

OCEANIA: It is a simple diode.

ASIATICA: Aha.

AFRICANII: Within are an anode and a cathode. The positive electrons travel from the cathode across voltage fields—

OCEANIA: The cathode is, in fact, negatively charged.

AFRICANII: No, positive, I I I I— *(She begins carefully to examine the works in the back of the radio)*

EUROPA: This device ought never to have been brought here. It is a Pandemonium.

AUSTRALIA: I I I I agree. In diodes we see manifest the selfsame Divided Human Consciousness which has engendered the multifarious catastrophes to which We are impotent witness. But—

AFRICANII *(Having concluded her examination, to Oceania)*: You are correct, it is negative. Regardless of the charge, it is the absence of resistance in a vacuum which—

ANTARCTICA: I I I do not weep for them, I I I weep for the vexation of the Blank Spaces, I I I weep for the Dancing Light, for the irremediable wastage of Fossil Fuels, Old Blood of the Globe spilled wantonly or burned and jettisoned into the Crystal Air—

AUSTRALIA: But it is a Conundrum, and We cannot solve Conundrums. If only He would return. I I I I do not know whether We have erred in transporting these dubious Inventions, but . . .

(Opening a huge dusty Book) If We refer to His Codex of Procedure, I I I I cannot recall which page but—

(There is an enormous peal of thunder and a blaze of lightning.
The Angel of America ushers Prior into the chamber. Terrified and determined, he stands before the council table.
The Principalities stare at Prior.)

ANGEL: Most August Fellow Principalities, Angels Most High: I regret my absence at this session, I was detained.

(Pause.)

AUSTRALIA: Ah, this is . . . ?
ANGEL: The Prophet. Yes.
AUSTRALIA: Ah.

(Exchanging brief, concerned glances with one another, the Angels bow to Prior.)

EUROPA: We were working.

AFRICANII: Making Progress.

(Thunderclap. Prior's startled. Then, realizing they're waiting for him to speak, he musters his courage and says in a small, uncertain voice:)

PRIOR: I . . . I want to return this.

(He holds out the Book. No one takes it from him.)

AUSTRALIA: What is the matter with it?

PRIOR: It just . . . It just . . .

(They wait, anxious to hear his explanation. A beat, then:)

PRIOR: We can't just stop. We're not rocks. Progress, migration, motion is . . . modernity. It's *animate*, it's what living things do. We desire. Even if all we desire is stillness, it's still desire *for*. *(On "for" he makes a motion with his hand: starting one place, moving forward)* Even if we go faster than we should. We can't *wait*. And wait for what? God—

(Thunderclap.)

PRIOR: God—

(Thunderclap.)

PRIOR: He isn't coming back.
     And even if He did . . .
     If He ever did come back, if He ever *dared* to show His face, or his Glyph or whatever in the Garden again. If after all this destruction, if after all the terrible days of

this terrible century He returned to see . . . how much suffering His abandonment had created, if all He has to offer is death . . .

You should *sue* the bastard. That's my only contribution to all this *Theology*. Sue the bastard for walking out. How dare He. He oughta pay.

(All stand, frozen, then the Angels exchange glances. Then:)

ANGEL: Thus spake the Prophet.

PRIOR *(Holding out the Book)*: So thank you . . . for sharing this with me, but I don't want to keep it.

OCEANIA: He wants to live.

PRIOR *(Grief breaking through)*: Yes! *(Pushing the sorrow back, determined to stay composed)* I'm thirty years old, for God-sake—

(A softer rumble of thunder.)

PRIOR: I haven't *done* anything yet, I—I want to be healthy again! And this plague, it should stop. In me and everywhere. Make it go away.

AUSTRALIA: Oh We have tried.
We suffer with You but
We do not know. We
Do not know how.

(Prior and Australia look at each other.)

EUROPA: This is the Tome of Immobility, of respite, of cessation.
Drink of its bitter water once, Prophet, and never thirst again.

PRIOR: I . . . can't.

(Prior puts the Book on the table. He removes his prophet robes, revealing the hospital gown underneath. He places the robe by the Book.)

PRIOR: I still want . . . My blessing. Even sick. I want to be alive.

ANGEL: You only think you do.
Life is a habit with you.
You have not *seen* what is to come:
We *have*:
What will the grim Unfolding of these Latter Days
    bring
That you or any Being should wish to endure them?
Death more plenteous than all Heaven has tears to
    mourn it,
The slow dissolving of the Great Design,
The spiraling apart of the Work of Eternity,
The World and its beautiful particle logic
All collapsed. All dead, forever,
In starless, moon-lorn onyx night.

(The Angel goes to Prior.)

ANGEL: We are failing, failing,
    The Earth and the Angels.
    Look up, look up.

(Prior and the Angel are looking up.)

ANGEL: It is Not-to-Be Time.

(The sound of the enormous generator begins to slow and then to fail. The lights in the chamber dim.)

141

ANGEL *(Asking Prior a real question, mystified by his persistence)*:
  Oh who asks of the Orders Blessing
  With Apocalypse Descending?
  Who demands: More Life
  When Death like a Protector Blinds our eyes,
    shielding from tender nerve
  More horror than can be borne?

  (She returns to stand with the other Principalities, all facing Prior.)

ANGEL: Let any Being on whom Fortune smiles
  Creep away to Death
  Before that last dreadful daybreak
  When all your ravaging returns to you
  With the rising, scorching, unrelenting Sun:
  When morning blisters crimson
  And bears all life away,
  A tidal wave of Protean Fire
  That curls around the planet
  And bares the Earth clean as bone.

  (Pause.)

PRIOR: But still. Still.
  Bless me anyway.
  I want more life. I can't help myself. I do.
  I've lived through such terrible times, and there are people who live through much much worse, but . . . You see them living anyway. When they're more spirit than body, more sores than skin, when they're burned and in agony, when flies lay eggs in the corners of the eyes of their children, they live. Death usually has to *take* life

away. I don't know if that's just the animal. I don't know if it's not braver to die. But I recognize the habit. The addiction to being alive. We live past hope. If I can find hope anywhere, that's it, that's the best I can do. It's so much not enough, so inadequate but . . . Bless me anyway. I want more life.

(He turns away to leave. When his back is turned, the Angels silently make mystical signs.

Prior stops, suddenly feeling sick again: leg pain, constricted lungs, cloudy vision, febrile panic and under that, dreadful weakness.

He gathers his strength, then turns again, with a new calm, to face them.)

PRIOR: You haven't seen what's to come. You've only seen what you're afraid is coming. Until it arrives—please don't be offended but . . . all you can see is fear.

I'm leaving Heaven to you now. I'll take my illness with me, and. And I'll take my death with me, too.

The earth's my home, and I want to go home.

Scene 6

Seven A.M. Prior descends from Heaven and slips into his hospital bed.

Belize is sleeping in a chair.

PRIOR *(Waking)*: Oh.
  I'm exhausted.
BELIZE *(Waking)*: You've been working hard.

PRIOR: I feel terrible.

BELIZE: Welcome back to the world.

PRIOR: From where, I . . .

Oh. Oh I—

(Emily enters.)

EMILY: Well look at this. It's the dawn of man.

BELIZE: Venus rising from the sea.

PRIOR: I'm wet.

EMILY: Fever broke. That's a good sign, they'll be in to change you in—

PRIOR *(Looking around)*: Mrs. Pitt? Did she—

BELIZE: Elle fait sa toilette. Elle est *tres* formidable, ça. Where did you find her?

PRIOR: We found each other, she—

I've had a remarkable dream. And *(To Belize)* you were there, and *(To Emily)* you.

(Hannah enters.)

PRIOR: And you.

HANNAH: I what?

PRIOR: And some of it was terrible, and some of it was wonderful, but all the same I kept saying I want to go home. And They sent me home.

HANNAH *(To Prior)*: What are you talking about?

PRIOR *(To Hannah)*: Thank you.

HANNAH: I just slept in the chair.

PRIOR *(To Belize)*: She saved my life.

HANNAH: I did no such thing, I slept in the chair. Being in hospital upsets me, it reminds me of things.

I have to go home now. I had the most *peculiar* dream.

(There's a knock on the door. It opens. Louis enters.)

LOUIS: Can I come in?

(Brief tense pause; Prior looks at Louis and then at Belize.)

EMILY: I have to start rounds.
> *(To Prior)* You're one of the lucky ones. I could give
> you a rose. You rest your weary bones.

PRIOR *(To Louis)*: What are you . . .
> *(He sees Louis's cuts and bruises)* What happened to *you?*

LOUIS: Visible scars. You said—

PRIOR: Oh, Louis, you're so goddamned literal about everything.

HANNAH *(A quick glance at Louis when Prior says his name, then)*:
I'm going now.

PRIOR: You'll come back.

HANNAH *(A beat, then)*: If I can. I have things to take care of.

PRIOR: Please do.
> I have always depended on the kindness of strangers.

HANNAH: Well that's a stupid thing to do.

(Hannah exits.)

LOUIS: Who's she?

PRIOR *(A beat, then)*: You really don't want to know.

BELIZE: Before I depart. A homecoming gift.

*(Belize puts his shoulder bag on Prior's lap. Prior opens it; it's
full of bottles of pills.)*

PRIOR *(Squinting hard)*: What? I can't read the label, I—
My eyes. Aren't any better.

(Squints even harder) AZT?
Where on earth did you . . . These are hot pills. I am shocked.

BELIZE: A contribution to the get-well fund. From a bad fairy.

LOUIS: These pills, they . . . They make you better.

PRIOR: They're poison, they make you anemic.
This is my life, from now on, Louis. I'm not getting "better."
(To Belize) I'm not sure I'm ready to do that to my bone marrow.

BELIZE *(Taking the bag)*: We can talk about it tomorrow. I'm going home to nurse my grudges. Ta, baby, sleep all day. Ta, Louis, you sure know how to clear a room.

(Belize exits.)

LOUIS: Prior.
I want to come back to you.

Scene 7

Same morning. Split scene: Louis and Prior in Prior's hospital room, continuous from Scene 6. Harper and Joe in Brooklyn. Joe sits in a chair; Harper enters from the bedroom, dressed for traveling, carrying a small suitcase.

HARPER: I want the credit card.
That's all. You can keep track of me from where the charges come from. If you want to keep track. I don't care.

JOE: I have some things to tell you.

HARPER: Oh we shouldn't talk. I don't want to do that anymore.

Credit card.

JOE: I don't know what will happen to me without you. Only
you. Only you love me. Out of everyone in the world.
I have done things, I'm ashamed. But I have changed.
I don't know how yet, but . . . Please, please, don't leave
me now.

Harper.

You're my good heart.

(She looks at him, she walks up to him and slaps him, hard.)

HARPER *(Quietly)*: Did that hurt?

(Joe nods yes.)

HARPER: Yes. Remember that. Please.

If I can get a job, or something, I'll cut the card to
pieces. And there won't be charges anymore. Credit card.

(Joe takes out his wallet, gives her the card.)

JOE: Call or . . . Call. You have to.

HARPER: No. Probably never again. That's how bad.

Sometimes, maybe lost is best. Get lost. Joe. Go
exploring.

*(Harper takes a bottle of Valium from a coat pocket. She
shakes out two pills, goes to Joe, takes his hand and puts the
Valium in his open palm.)*

HARPER: With a big glass of water.

(Harper leaves.)

LOUIS: I want to come back to you.

You could . . . respond, you could say something, throw me out or say it's fine, or it's not fine but sure what the hell or . . .

(Little pause)

I really failed you. But . . . This is hard. Failing in love isn't the same as not loving. It doesn't let you off the hook, it doesn't mean . . . you're free to not love.

PRIOR: I love you Louis.

LOUIS: Good. I love you.

PRIOR: I really do.

But you can't come back. Not ever.

I'm sorry. But you can't.

Scene 8

That night. Louis and Prior remain from the previous scene. Joe is sitting alone in Brooklyn. Harper appears. She is in a window seat on board a jumbo jet, airborne.

HARPER: Night flight to San Francisco. Chase the moon across America. God! It's been years since I was on a plane!

When we hit thirty-five-thousand feet, we'll have reached the tropopause. The great belt of calm air. As close as I'll ever get to the ozone.

I dreamed we were there. The plane leapt the tropopause, the safe air, and attained the outer rim, the ozone, which was ragged and torn, patches of it threadbare as old cheesecloth, and that was frightening . . .

But I saw something only I could see, because of my astonishing ability to see such things:

Souls were rising, from the earth far below, souls of the dead, of people who had perished, from famine, from war, from the plague, and they floated up, like skydivers in reverse, limbs all akimbo, wheeling and spinning. And the souls of these departed joined hands, clasped ankles, and formed a web, a great net of souls, and the souls were three-atom oxygen molecules, of the stuff of ozone, and the outer rim absorbed them, and was repaired.

Nothing's lost forever. In this world, there is a kind of painful progress. Longing for what we've left behind, and dreaming ahead.

At least I think that's so.

Bethesda

January 1990

Prior, Louis, Belize and Hannah sitting on the rim of the Bethesda Fountain in Central Park. It's a bright day, but cold.
   Prior is heavily bundled, and he has thick glasses on. He supports himself with a cane. Hannah is noticeably different—she looks like a New Yorker, and she's reading an issue of The Nation. *Louis and Belize are arguing. The Bethesda Angel is above them all.*

LOUIS: The Berlin Wall has fallen. The Ceauşescus are out. He's building democratic socialism. The New Internationalism. Gorbachev is the greatest political thinker since Lenin.

BELIZE: I don't think we know enough yet to start canonizing him. The Russians hate his guts.

LOUIS: Yeah but. Remember back four years ago? The whole time we were feeling everything everywhere was stuck, while in Russia! Look! Perestroika! The Thaw! It's the end of the Cold War! The whole world is changing! Overnight!

HANNAH: I wonder what'll happen now in places like Yugo-slavia.

LOUIS: Yugoslavia?

PRIOR *(To audience)*: Let's just turn the volume down on this, OK?

They'll be at it for hours. It's not that what they're saying isn't important, it's just . . .

This is my favorite place in New York City. No, in the whole universe. The parts of it I have seen.

On a day like today. A sunny winter's day, warm and cold at once. The sky's a little hazy, so the sunlight has a physical presence, a character. In autumn, those trees across the lake are yellow, and the sun strikes those most brilliantly. Against the blue of the sky, that sad fall blue, those trees are more light than vegetation. They are Yankee trees, New England transplants. They're barren now.

It's January 1990. I've been living with AIDS for five years. That's six whole months longer than I lived with Louis.

LOUIS: Whatever comes, what you have to admire in Gorbachev, in the Russians is that they're making a leap into the unknown. You can't wait around for a theory. The sprawl of life, the weird . . .

HANNAH: Interconnectedness.

LOUIS: Yes.

BELIZE: Maybe the sheer size of the terrain.

LOUIS: It's all too much to be encompassed by a single theory now.

BELIZE: The world is faster than the mind.

LOUIS: That's what politics is. The world moving ahead. And only in politics does the miraculous occur.

BELIZE: But that's a theory.

HANNAH: You can't live in the world without an idea of the world, but it's living that makes the ideas. You can't wait for a theory, but you have to have a theory.

LOUIS: Go know. As my grandma would say.

PRIOR *(Turning the sound off again)*: This angel. She's my favorite angel. I like them best when they're statuary. They commemorate death but they suggest a world without dying. They are made of the heaviest things on earth, stone and iron, they weigh tons but they're winged, they are engines and instruments of flight.

This is the angel Bethesda. Louis will tell you her story.

LOUIS: Oh. Um, well, she was this angel, she landed in the Temple Square in Jerusalem, in the days of the Second Temple, right in the middle of a working day she descended and just her foot touched earth. And where it did, a fountain shot up from the ground.

When the Romans destroyed the Temple, the fountain of Bethesda ran dry.

PRIOR: And Belize will tell you about the nature of the fountain, before its flowing stopped.

BELIZE: If anyone who was suffering, in the body or the spirit, walked through the waters of the fountain of Bethesda, they would be healed, washed clean of pain.

PRIOR: They know this because I've told them, many times. Hannah here told it to me. She also told me this:

HANNAH: When the Millennium comes—

PRIOR: Not the year two thousand, but the capital-M Millennium—

HANNAH: Right. The fountain of Bethesda will flow again. And I told him I would personally take him there to bathe. We will all bathe ourselves clean.

LOUIS: Not literally in Jerusalem, I mean we don't want this to have sort of Zionist implications, we—

BELIZE: Right on.

LOUIS: But on the other hand we *do* recognize the right of the state of Israel to exist.

BELIZE: But the West Bank should be a homeland for the Palestinians, and the Golan Heights should—

LOUIS: Well not *both* the West Bank and the Golan Heights, I mean no one supports Palestinian rights more than I do but—

BELIZE: Oh yeah right, Louis, like not even the Palestinians are more devoted than—

PRIOR: I'm almost done.

The fountain's not flowing now, they turn it off in the winter, ice in the pipes. But in the summer it's a sight to see. I want to be around to see it. I plan to be. I hope to be.

This disease will be the end of many of us, but not nearly all, and the dead will be commemorated and will struggle on with the living, and we are not going away. We won't die secret deaths anymore. The world only spins forward. We will be citizens. The time has come.

Bye now.

You are fabulous creatures, each and every one.

And I bless you: *More Life.*

The Great Work Begins.

END OF PLAY

Two Omitted Scenes from Perestroika

In previous published versions of *Perestroika* I included two scenes which were almost always cut in production. In preparing this new version, I decided it was time to acknowledge the verdict of twenty-two years of production history and remove the scenes from the play. I'm including them here for whatever enjoyment and interest they provide readers; the play in production unquestionably works better without them.

This scene, formerly Act Five, Scene 6, immediately followed the scene in which Prior confronts the Angels in the Hall of the Principalities.

Act Five, Scene 6

On the streets of Heaven. Rabbi Isidor Chemelwitz and Sarah Ironson are seated on wooden crates with another crate between them. They are playing cards. Prior enters.

PRIOR: Excuse me, I'm looking for a way out of this, do . . .
Oh! You're . . .

SARAH IRONSON *(To the Rabbi)*: Vos vil er? [What does he
want?]

RABBI ISIDOR CHEMELWITZ: Di goyim, zey veysn nisht vi zikh
oyftsufirn. [These Gentiles, they have no manners.]

PRIOR: Are you Sarah Ironson?

(She looks up at him.)

PRIOR: I was at your funeral! You look just like your grandson,
Louis. I know him. Louis. He never wanted you to find
out, but did you know he's gay?

SARAH IRONSON *(Not understanding)*: Vi? [What?]

RABBI ISIDOR CHEMELWITZ: Dein aynickl, Louis? [Your
grandson, Louis?]

SARAH IRONSON: Yeah?

RABBI ISIDOR CHEMELWITZ *(Sotto voce)*: Er iz a feygele.

SARAH IRONSON: A *feygele*? Oy.

RABBI ISIDOR CHEMELWITZ *(To Sarah)*: Itst gistu. [You deal.]

PRIOR: Why does everyone here play cards?

RABBI ISIDOR CHEMELWITZ: Why? *(To Sarah)* Dos goy vil
visnfar-Vos mir shpiln in kortn. [The goy wants to know
why we play cards.]

OK.

Cards is strategy but mostly a game of chance. In
Heaven, everything is known. To the Great Questions
are lying about here like yesterday's newspaper all the
answers. So from what comes the pleasures of Paradise?
Indeterminacy! Because mister, with the Angels, may
their names be always worshipped and adored, it's all
gloom and doom and give up already. But still is there
Accident, in this pack of playing cards, still is there the

Unknown, the Future. You understand me? It ain't all so much mechanical as they think.

You got another question?

PRIOR: I want to go home.

RABBI ISIDOR CHEMELWITZ: Oh simple. Here. To do this, every Kabbalist on earth would sell his right nut.

Penuel, Peniel, Ja'akov Beth-Yisroel, Killeeyou, kill-eemee, OOO-ooooooo-OOOO-oooooohmayn!

(The ladder, the music and the lights. Prior starts to descend.)

SARAH IRONSON: Hey! Zogt Loubeleh az di Bobbe zogt:

RABBI ISIDOR CHEMELWITZ: She says tell this Louis Grandma says:

SARAH IRONSON: Er iz tomid geven a bissele farblonjet, shoin vi a boytshikl. Ober siz nisht keyn antshuldigunk.

RABBI ISIDOR CHEMELWITZ: From when he was a boy he was always mixed up. But it's no excuse.

SARAH IRONSON: *He should have visited!* But I forgive. Tell him: az er darf ringen mit zain Libm Nomen. Yah?!

RABBI ISIDOR CHEMELWITZ: You should struggle with the Almighty.

SARAH IRONSON: Azoi toot a Yid.

RABBI ISIDOR CHEMELWITZ: It's the Jewish way.

END OF SCENE

Two Omitted Scenes

In earlier versions of *Perestroika*'s Act Five, this scene followed Scene 7 and preceded Scene 8 (in the current version's numbering).

Roy, in Heaven, or Hell or Purgatory—standing waist-deep in a smoldering pit, facing a great flaming Aleph, which bathes him and the whole theater in a volcanic, pulsating red light. Underneath, a basso-profundo roar, like a thousand Bessemer furnaces going at once, deep underground.

ROY: Paternity suit? Abandonment? Family court is my particular metier, I'm an absolute fucking demon with Family Law. Just tell me who the judge is, and what kind of jewelry does he like? If it's a jury, it's harder, juries take more talk but sometimes it's worth it, going jury, for what it saves you in bribes. Yes I will represent you, King of the Universe, yes I will sing and eviscerate, I will bully and seduce, I will win for you and make the plaintiffs, those traitors, wish they had never heard the name of . . .
   (Huge thunderclap)
   Is it a done deal, are we on? Good, then I gotta start by telling you you ain't got a case here, you're guilty as hell, no question, you have nothing to plead but not to worry, darling, I will make something up.

END OF SCENE

A Few Notes from the Playwright About Staging

In General

Millennium Approaches and *Perestroika* are two parts of a single play, but at the same time they're two rather different plays, each with its own structure and character. *Millennium* has three acts and *Perestroika* has five. Three acts make a tauter, cleaner play, the gestures and rhythms of which will feel more inexorable, more destination-driven; a five-act play is likely to provide a more expansive, exploratory and ultimately openended and unresolved experience. Perhaps it can be said that *Millennium* is a play about security and certainty being blown apart, while *Perestroika* is about danger and possibility following the explosion. The events in *Perestroika* proceed from the wreckage made by the Angel's traumatic entry at the end of *Millennium*. A membrane has broken; there is disarray and debris. All of which is to suggest that, especially when the

159

two parts of *Angels* are produced in repertory, the differences should be visible and palpable onstage.

The plays benefit from a pared-down style of presentation, with scenery kept to an evocative and informative minimum. There are a lot of scenes and a lot of locations; an informative minimum means providing what's needed to enable the audience to know, as quickly as possible, where a scene is set. Actors need to help by playing the reality of these locations: How loud can you get, really, in a fancy restaurant?

I recommend rapid scene shifts (no blackouts!), employing the cast as well as stagehands in shifting the scene. This must be an actor-driven event.

Intermissions

Audiences are said to have grown increasingly impatient and unwilling to sit through long evenings in the theater. The people of whom this is true will likely seek out shorter plays than *Angels in America*. I believe that, once engaged, audiences rediscover the rewards of patience and effort and the pleasures of an epic journey. An epic play *should* be a little fatiguing; a rich, heady, hard-earned fatigue is among a long journey's pleasures and rewards.

That said, the audience has to be given chances along the way to gather its strength and attention. *Millennium Approaches* is a long play, and *Perestroika* is longer. Each play is meant to have two intermissions, after Act One and Act Two of *Millennium*, and after Act Three and Act Four of *Perestroika*. These segments are shaped to function as coherent single events as well as successions of scenes.

The temptation to take only one intermission in each of the two parts should, in my opinion, be resisted. Although one intermission shortens the running time, the demands it puts on the audience's attention and the pressures it puts on the scenes immediately before the single intermission or near the end of the play are unnecessary, detrimental and counter-productive—the running time may be shorter, but it will feel much longer.

Magic

The moments of magic, such as the appearance and disappearance of Mr. Lies, the ghosts, Prior's fiery Book hallucination and the Angel's arrival, ought to be fully imagined and realized, as wonderful *theatrical* illusions—which means it's OK if the wires show, and maybe it's good that they do, but the magic should at the same time be thoroughly thrilling, fantastical, amazing.

It's easy to stage a person's (or a ghost's) magical disappearance by simply having the actor exit into the wings, but I don't think that's a strong choice. Not only is it *not* thoroughly thrilling, fantastical, amazing or fun to watch a person walk offstage, it's also pedestrian, literally and figuratively. Walking offstage is slow, and therefore it lacks one very important aspect of *vanishing*—namely that it's abrupt. In a world in which young people by their thousands sicken and, with obscene speed, die (in other words, the world of this play), vanishing abruptly is particularly upsetting, even frightening. The magic ought to be fun for the audience, but also disturbing. For Prior, it's increasingly terrifying.

There's more magic in *Perestroika*, and as the play progresses, the magic gets grander. It's hard to make this happen: long, two-part plays are enormously demanding of resources, time and energy, and there's always the risk that invention, attention to detail, time and cash will run out just when they're needed most, in the play's home stretch. *Perestroika*'s fifth-act Heaven scenes should, whether or not the stage directions are followed, at the very least resemble nothing on Earth; the Hall of the Continental Principalities in Act Five, Scene 5, ought to be the high point of the stage magic of *Angels*.

Split Scenes

In the split scenes, two separate events occur more or less simultaneously in different locations—for example, Act One, Scene 8, of *Millennium Approaches*, in which we observe Harper and Joe in their living room in Brooklyn and Louis and Prior in their Alphabetland bedroom. Both events are intended to continue, active and alive, throughout the entire split scene, with focus going where the story needs it to go. Stopping one of the two events in its tracks by artificially freezing it is an easy but again, in my opinion, not a strong choice. The trick is to work out psychologically coherent (hence playable), compellingly dramatic reasons why the characters in one event become still and quiet when the action that the audience should be attending to shifts to the other event and onto other characters.

When a character chooses to stop talking, to be still and quiet, for reasons having to do with the conflict he or she is in during a scene, an active choice is being made, and hence the character stays alive onstage—as opposed to being put in suspended animation by the director. Finding concurrent, complementary vitality in the two events of a split scene gives them their particular dynamism; they'll be much more fun to play, and to watch.

Language

The engine of the play is the struggle in which the characters engage to change unendurable circumstances—*all* the characters, *all* the time we're watching them. The circumstances the characters face, the world they inhabit, and the characters themselves are in a very important sense made up of words.

Words are important, and they're specific. We speak to produce effects, to catalyze, to engender consequences. We choose words strategically, precisely, whether or not we do so consciously.

If the character you're playing says something that strikes you, the actor, as odd, large, artificial, you should assume it strikes your character that way as well. If a character opposite yours says something that sounds ornate, awkward, a non-sequitur to you, the actor, it probably sounds that way to your character too.

I advise taking very seriously and working hard to answer the question that you, the actor, and probably also the character you're playing, are longing to ask: Why am I/Why is this other person talking this way? That question is important. When the language in the play is strange, in other words, its strangeness is always an action. A sentence is no less an action than a blow with a broadsword or a passionate kiss. And the degree and kind of strangeness matter enormously.

The characters in the play are fighting for survival; the stakes are very high. They talk to make things happen, to advance an agenda, to defend, to enlist, to seduce, to punish. Sometimes they speak in an effort to understand how or what they're feeling. But never speak solely to announce your character's distress, hoping for pity. The characters in the play are tougher than that; the world of the play, like the world outside the theater, is a tough place.

Two Notes Regarding Pronunciation

On page 20, Roy's coinage, "azido-methatalo-molamoca-whatchamacallit" is pronounced "aZIDOmuhTHATUHLO-moluhmocuh-whatchamacallit." The "I" in "ZIDO" is short, as in "in," and the "TH" in "*THA*TUHLO" is soft, as in "*TH*istle."

On page 88, Prior is using the verb "prophesy," which is pronounced "proph-uh-sigh," *not* the noun "prophecy" which is pronounced "proph-uh-see."

Nine Notes Regarding the Angel

The Angel, who is related to humans but isn't human, is arguably the most challenging character in *Angels*, and Act Two of *Perestroika* is inarguably the most challenging sequence. After two decades of struggling with her and watching others struggle, I'm offering these thoughts, which I hope will be helpful.

1) *Metaphysics:* I'll begin by repeating: The Angel is related to humans but isn't human. That's the primary challenge in acting, directing and designing her. For starters, she refers to herself in the plural (I I I I) because she isn't a single thing: She is a Principality, which is, depending on which angelological ordering system you subscribe to, the highest or one of the highest types among the angelic orders. She is four Divine Emanations—Lumen (blue), Candle (gold), Phosphor (green) and Fluor (purple)—manifest as an aggregate entity, the Continental Principality of America. I have no advice about how to play four nonhuman beings amalgamated into one nonhuman being. I only know that while she should be comprehensible to the audience, she should also be terribly unfamiliar.

2) *Appearance:* She should be extraordinary to behold, and her wings are of paramount importance—they should move and they should move us. She shouldn't look like Botticelli painted her, or any other Italian Renaissance painter, or any European of any period, or like a traditional Christmas tree ornament. She should look breathtaking, severe, scary, powerful, and magnificently American.

3) *Her Cough:* The Angel's cough is a manifestation of cosmic unwellness, but she controls it, and she is a creature of unimaginable strength and discipline. She doesn't want Prior to sense any weakness, disorder or confusion on her part, and her cough ought to be a single, dry bark, *not* prolonged wracking emphysemic spasms. Ellen McLaughlin, who created the role, based her brusque, even angry rap of a cough on a cat hacking up a furball. It was startling, sharp, simple—one *hack*, not ten—and effectively nonhuman, not funny as much as disconcerting and ominous, and always always *dignified*. It did not make her seem frail.

4) *She's Not Joking, and She's No Joke:* Some of what happens between Prior and the Angel is supposed to be funny, but it's essential for the play, and, for that matter, for the comedy, that the Angel's dignity and her unequivocally serious purpose are never—as in *not for one single second!*—compromised by schticky winking at the audience. Prior's terror at being in her presence and/or at the possibility that he's going mad never (as in not for one single second) abandons him. As Prior has his first full encounter with the Angel, and simultaneously relates it to Belize three weeks later, we're watching a cosmically high-stakes encounter between a badly frightened but very brave human being and his furious, grief-stricken, frightened and frighteningly powerful nonhuman visitor/intruder.

Apologies if I'm sounding strident, but I've learned that there are dire consequences if this reality is parodied or traduced. People can enjoy pratfalls, mugging and easy laughs, even while determining that they won't be fooled again into deep investment in what's proved to be unserious. Once faith in the seriousness of what's onstage has been withdrawn, however briefly, it's unlikely to return fully.

5) *Her Arrival:* If at all technically feasible, the Angel should arrive in Prior's bedroom by crashing through the ceiling. This is harder than bringing her through a crack in the rear wall, which is what's usually done. But she's coming down from Heaven, not from across town; it's a drop-down-on-your-head explosive revelation, rather than the sneaky, sideways kind. If at all possible, she should arrive in dust and noise as the ceiling rains down on Prior's head. I didn't know, when I wrote the play, that so few theaters have fly space.

6) *Flying Versus Rehearsing*: I also didn't know how difficult stage flying would prove to be. Originally I imagined that the Angel would fly during Act Two of *Perestroika*, doing spectacular aerial stunts as she spoke. I've seen many productions of *Perestroika*, and I've never seen this happen. What I've seen instead is many valuable hours of rehearsal and tech time lost, and much money spent hiring stage-flying specialists, trying to make this happen.

I've come to the conviction that attempting extensive flying is not only unwise, because it lies beyond the technical and temporal means of most theaters, it's a distraction from the real business at hand. The Anti-Migratory Epistle sequence in Act Two won't be solved by Angelic midair somersaults—which, trust me, will never materialize. The effectiveness of this long and difficult scene depends entirely on getting its complex realities clear, specific and playable, and that means time-consuming, painstaking, actor-director rehearsal-room work, for which there is no substitute.

7) *Unhooking the Angel:* There *should* be flying, of course: The Angel should fly in, and fly out, carrying the Epistle. In between her entrance and her exit, she has to be able to move around the stage, so that she can interact fully with Prior and, when appropriate, with Belize. This most likely means that she will have to be unhooked from her flying rig onstage while the scene is in progress, and then hooked back up. Stagehands, visible to the audience, can do this. Her fly-wires show, so why not visible stagehands? Stagehands ought to help Prior out of his prophet garb and into his pajamas in the transition from the street to his bedroom and back again.

Openly including the crew in the stage life in Act Two (when necessary for the storytelling, not as an embellishment) seems to me consonant with the act's mixing narrated and dramatized storytelling, an amalgam which occurs at no other point in *Angels.* Moments when the crew takes active part in the dramatic event should be staged—interesting to watch, specific and unapologetic, not artificially slow but not rushed and frantic. Prior's change of clothes, from prophet drag to pajamas, is part of a transition he's chosen to undertake. He's stepping into a violent memory because telling Belize isn't enough; Prior has to show him. When the stagehands unhook the Angel, they should do so respectfully; it goes without saying that they wouldn't touch her without her willing them to do so.

8) *Staging the Anti-Migratory Epistle:* Act Two confronts directors, actors and designers with the formidable (but, I hope, exciting and enjoyable) challenge of staging three characters

occupying two locations that are separated, albeit permeably and not cleanly, by distance and time.

This is a scene involving *three* characters: Prior, the Angel and Belize. There's a temptation to sideline Belize to a stationary spot on the outskirts and leave him there for the duration, tossing in quips, irrelevant to the action. This is a tempting choice because it makes the scene easier to stage. The problem is that without Belize's active involvement, the scene makes no sense. The overarching actions are the Angel's arrival, the delivery of the Epistle, Prior's refusal of it, and then his unwilling acceptance of or forced submission to it. But the scene takes place in the present as well as in the past, and integral to the event is the in-the-bedroom/on-the-street contest between Belize and the Angel for Prior's attention and soul, a battle of three strong wills that propels/pulls Belize into Prior's bedroom, into his awful dream—where, once he's entered, the Angel seems intermittently to be aware of Belize's presence.

Belize is tough, but Prior unfolds for him what must sound, to a nurse with considerable experience dealing with AIDS, like a wholly unfamiliar form of dementia, far more coherent than anything Belize has heard from his patients. He's bewildered, grief-stricken, and, when Prior's delusions assume uncharacteristically, deeply disturbing reactionary, even racist overtones, Belize becomes frightened and then angry. Thus Prior's desperate attempt to end his loneliness by telling his best friend about the waking nightmare in which he's trapped results in even greater isolation.

9) *Her Broken Heart:* The Angel's power and purpose semi-successfully conceal an abandoned lover's determination to get her lost love to return before everything falls apart. Prior is supposed to be useful, as surrogate for his species, the last fragile hope of averting universal extinction. But to the heart-

broken lover that this heavenly emissary also is, he's a hateful, guilty homewrecker who also happens to be her kin and her ward. In this predicament the Angel is recognizable to Prior, to Belize and to us, and she grows more familiar as the Epistle progresses, but only to a point. As I began, so I'll end: the Angel isn't human.